The Temple of the Unknown Craftswomen

In this art book I have transmuted my paintings off goddesses using AI to museum like artefacts. Turning some in to tapestry and embroidery digital images. The potentiality of AI and technology interests me. Inspired by the Textile work that didn't survive because of the degradability properties of the material. Therefore it isn't reflected in the archeological record. A medium typically utilised by women. Unlike male dominated mediums such as paintings and sculptures which allowed a one sided history to be archived, preserved and restored. The work I've created is out of the unknown it's fast and unskilled by using the skill of modern technology. The copious amounts of online images generated daily reflects how lost the images are in the world. It reflects the unpreserved history work of women's work and the 99% of art that is produced, bad, unknown and unrecognised.

The Image on the front cover is a Mortuary Temple of Hatshepsut, the temple was built in 1490 B.C. in Luxor. I visited this impressive temple on my travels in Egypt. The Egyptians also called these mansions of millions of years. Which I find interesting as it connects life to the afterlife much like museums and art. The work lives on like the temple of a woman king, called a king and wore a beard to be accepted. Much like women whom participated in art practice throughout history being advised to dress in trousers at a time when trousers were exclusively for men and adapting there name to a masculine one. Like Parisian bohemian artist Marie-Clémentine Valadon who used the name Suzanne Valadon. Suzanne started out as muse but by watching the male artists work she learnt skills while earning and started to paint herself from her own gaze. With her most iconic painting The Blue Room (*La chambre bleue*), 1923. Today women that want to be taken seriously need to conform to the male dominated world if they have a masculine style, personality and have the luxury to be born genetically and hormonally more compliant to the characteristics similar to males.

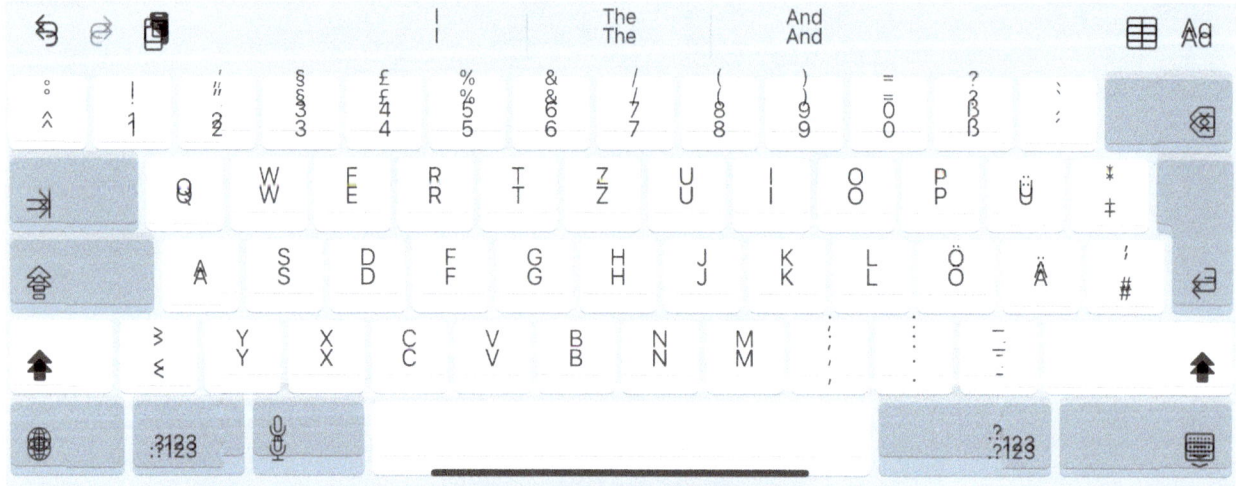

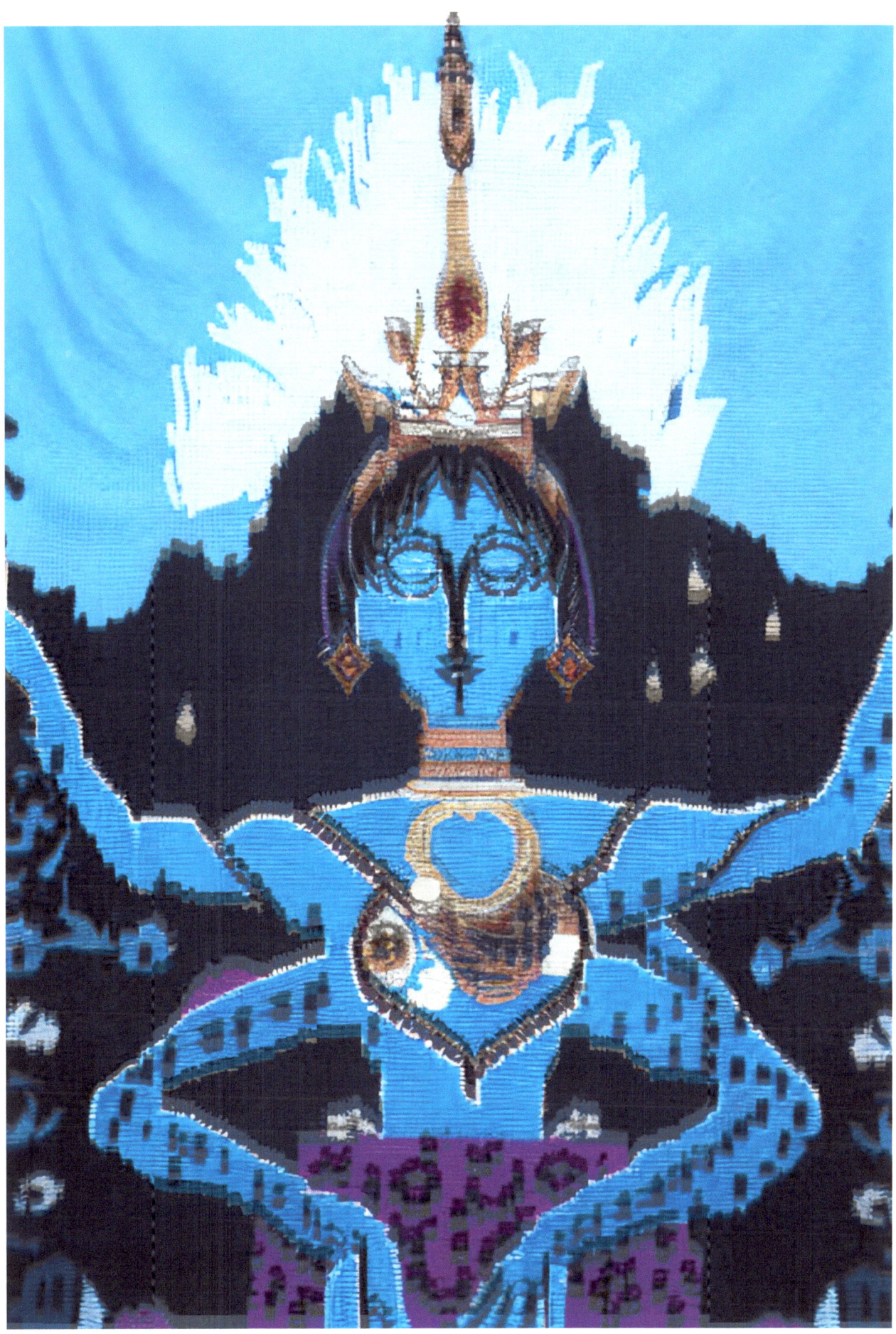

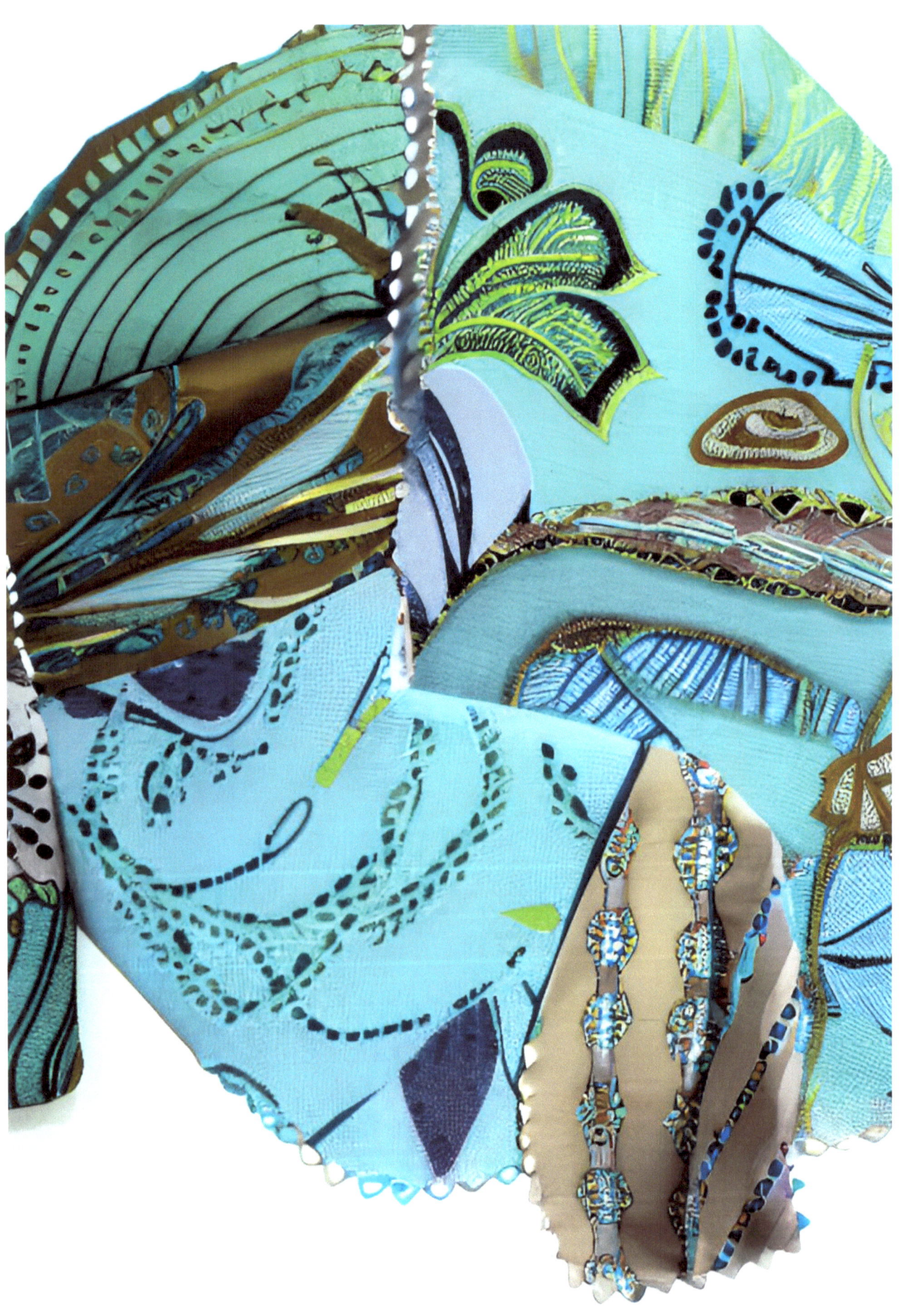

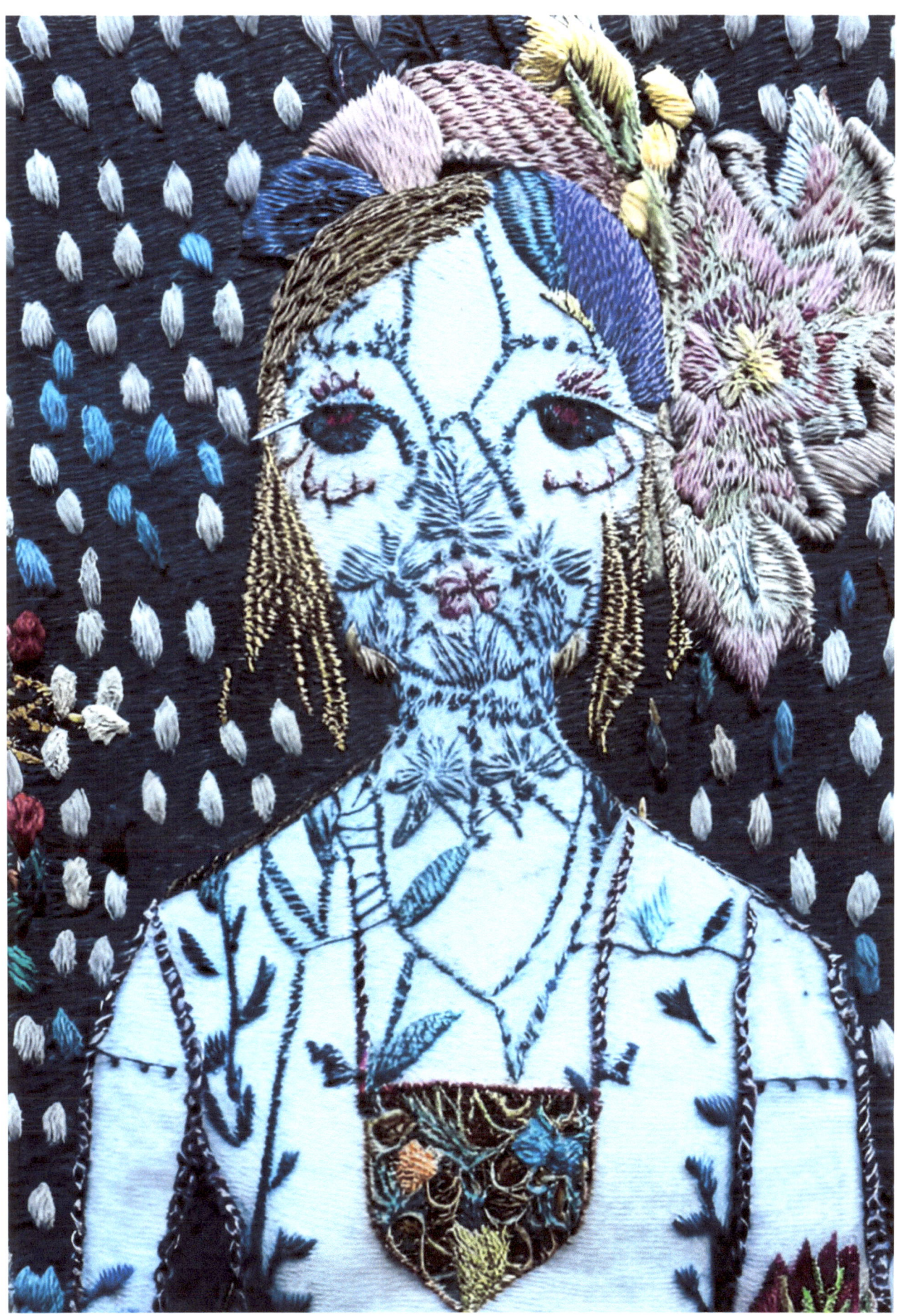

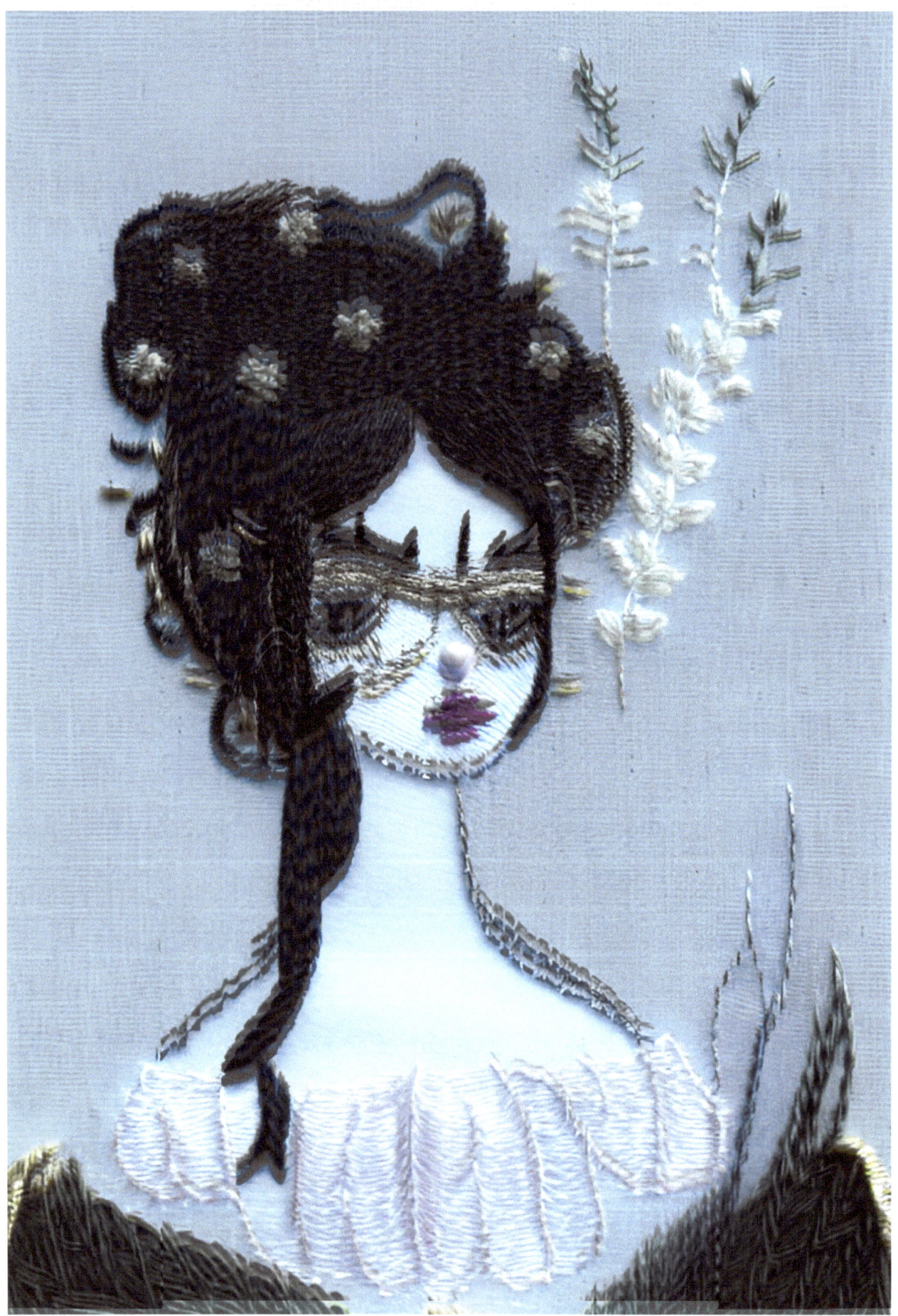

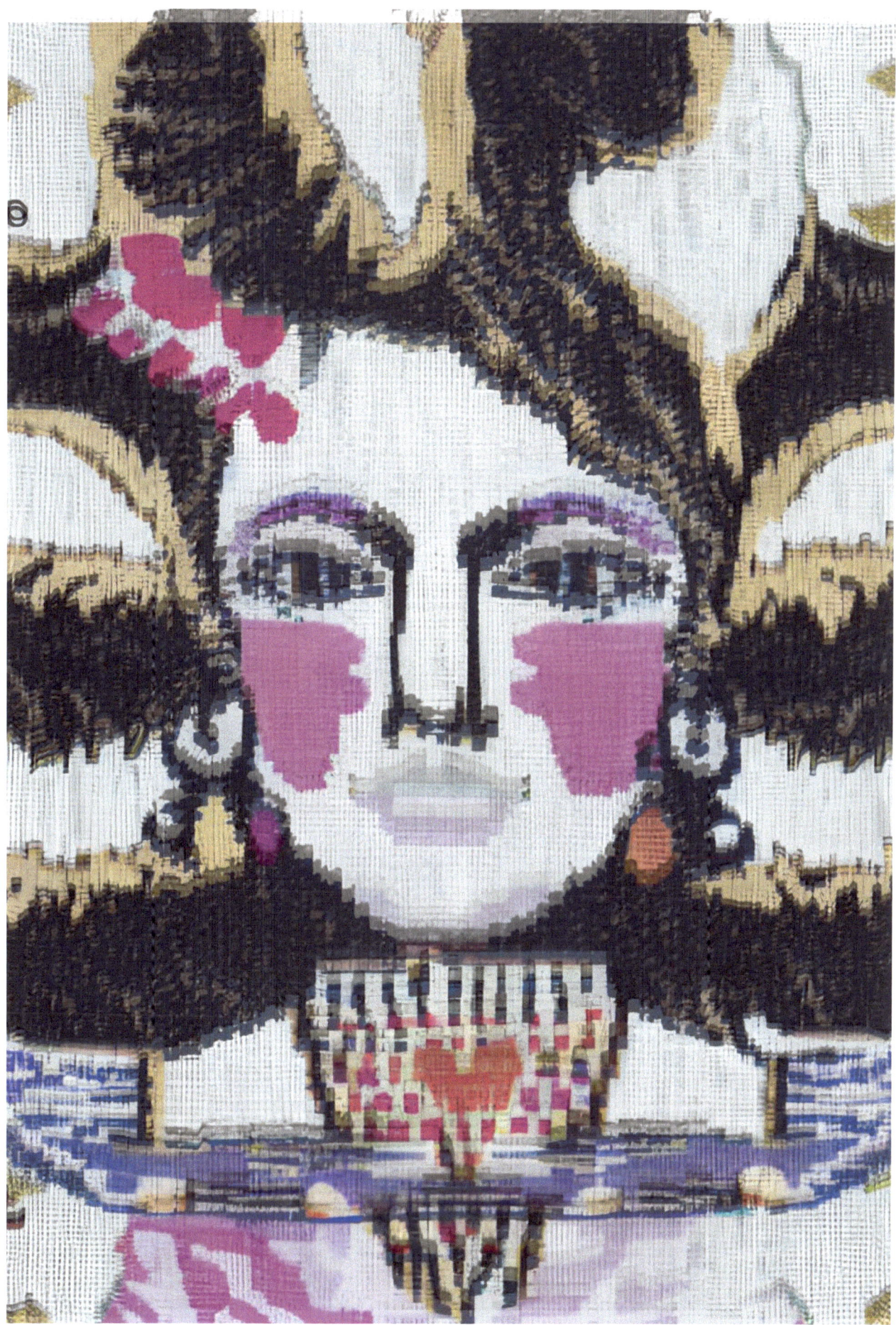

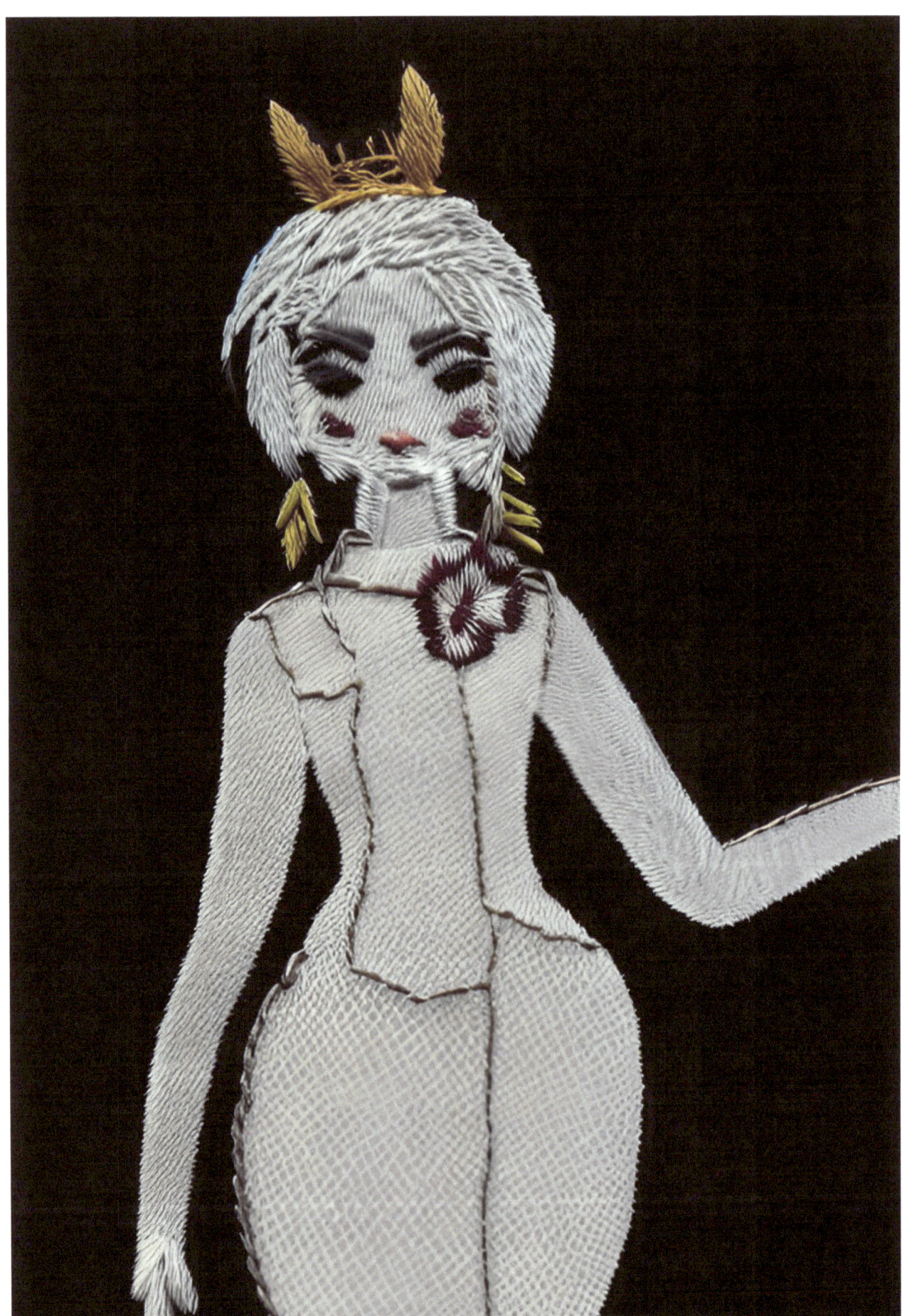

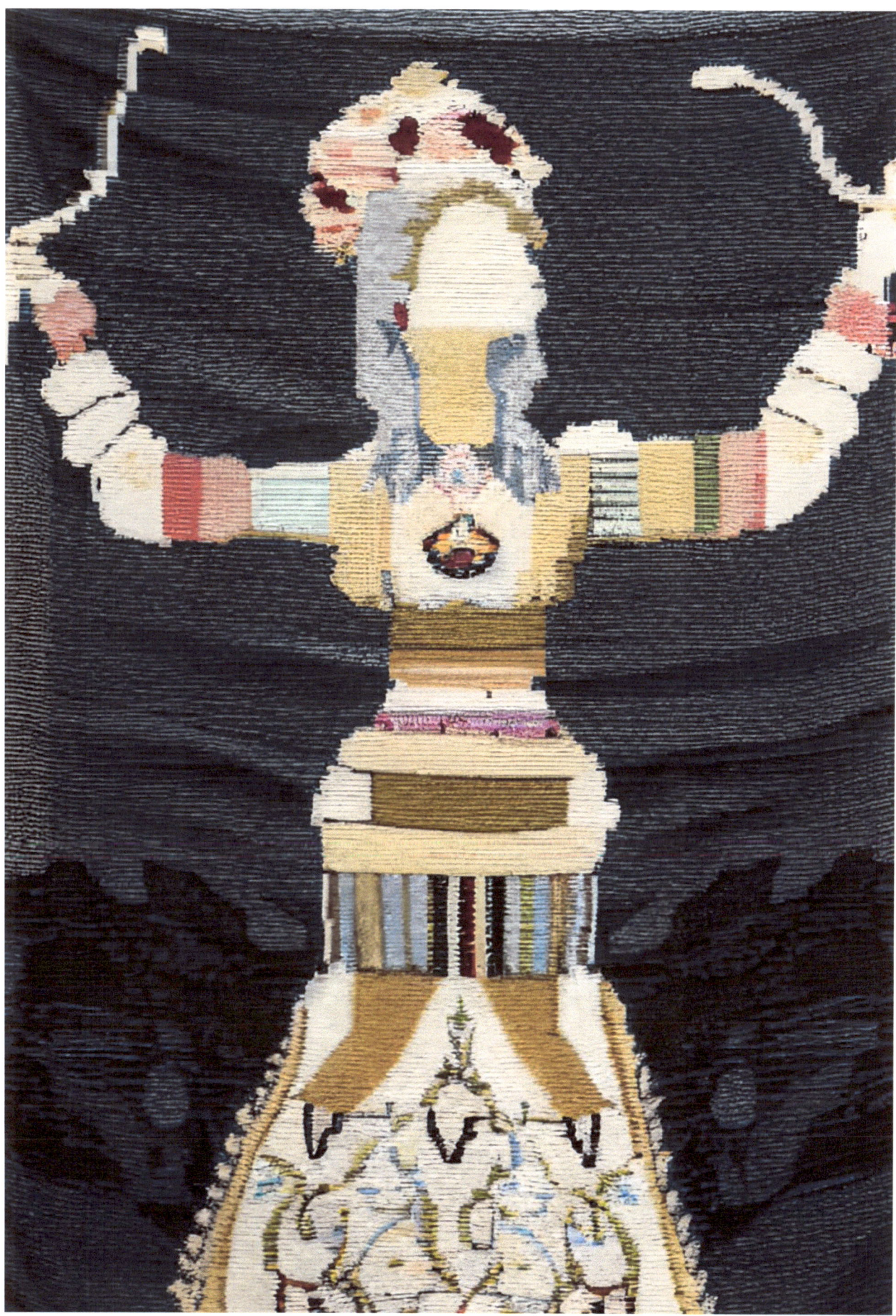

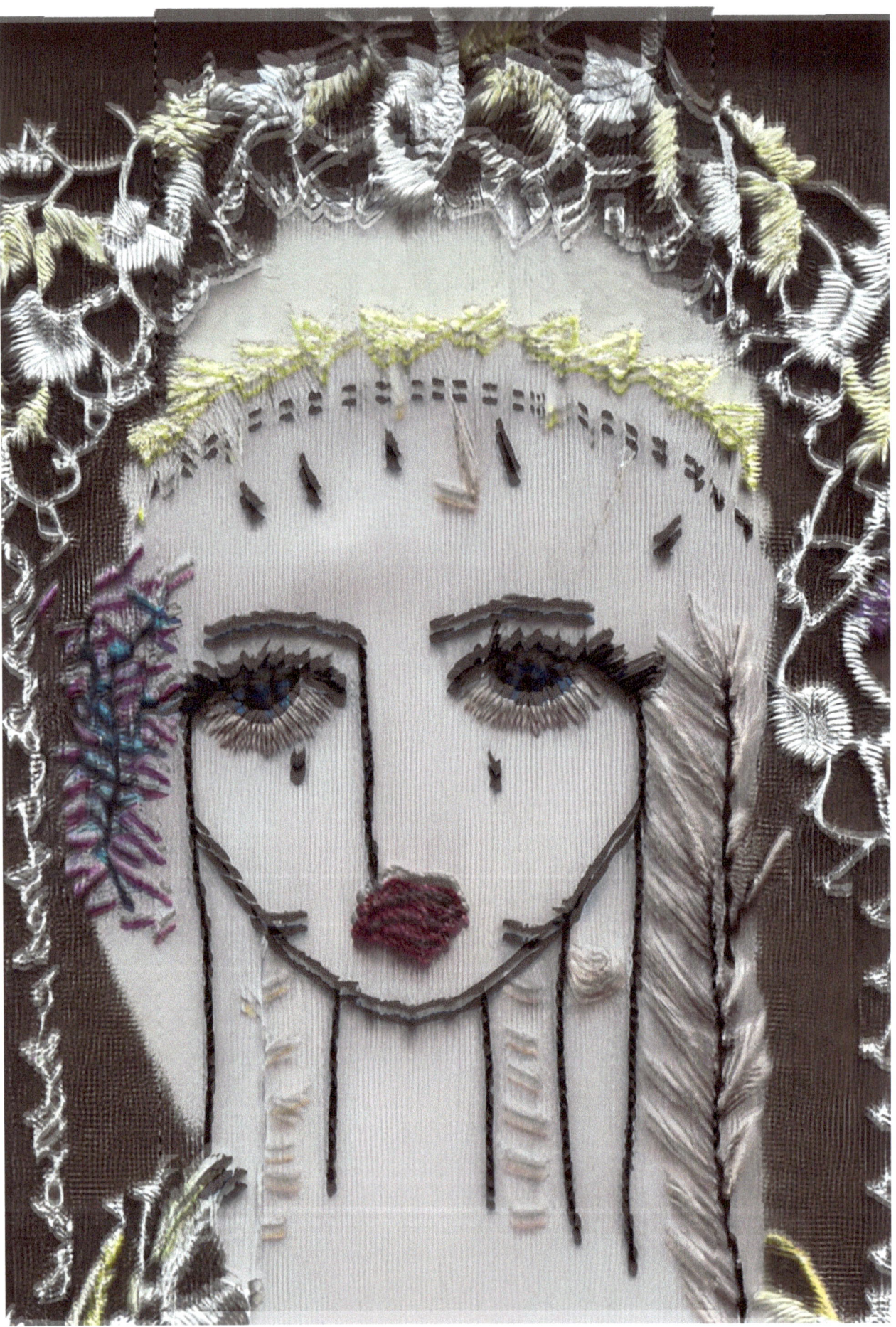

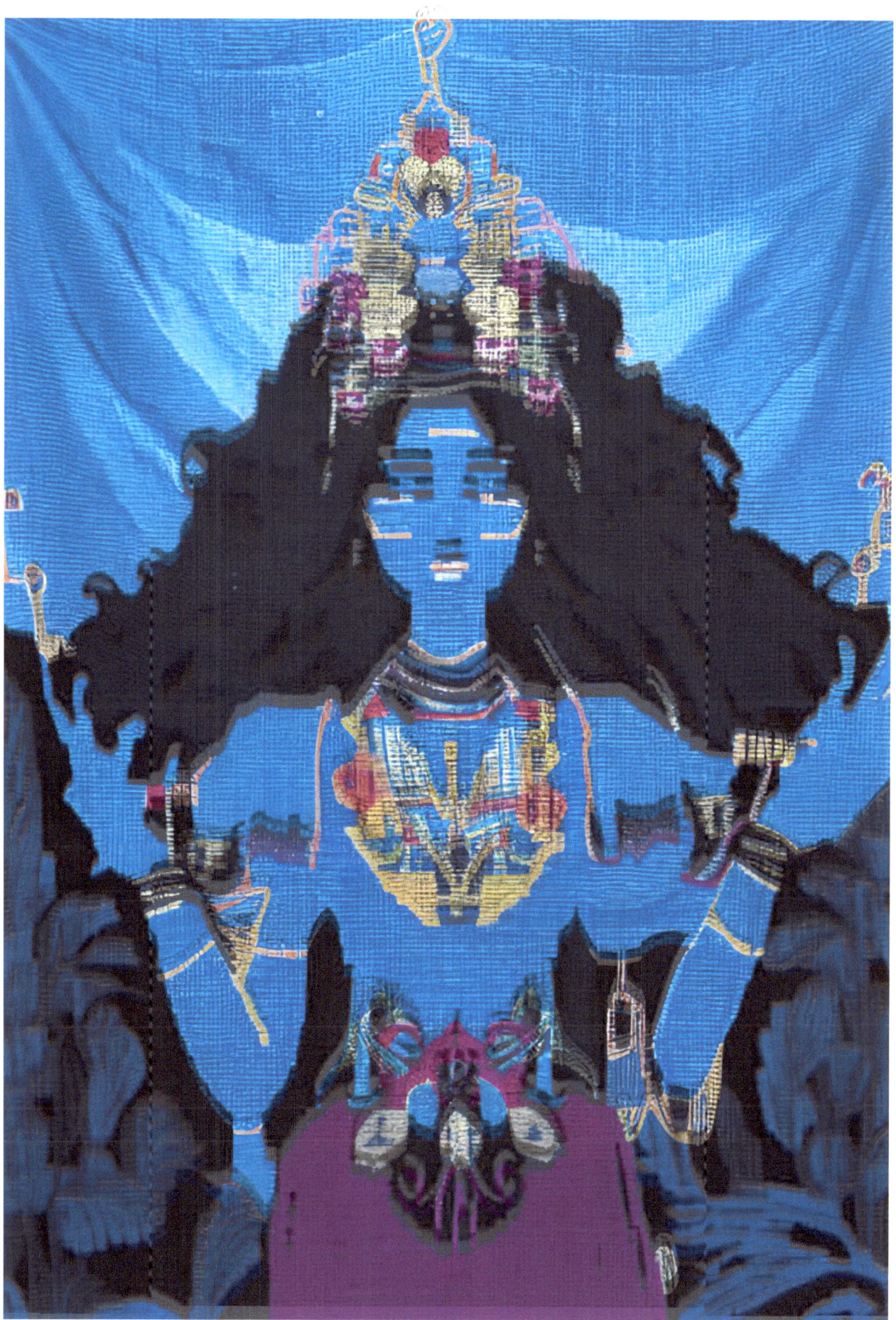

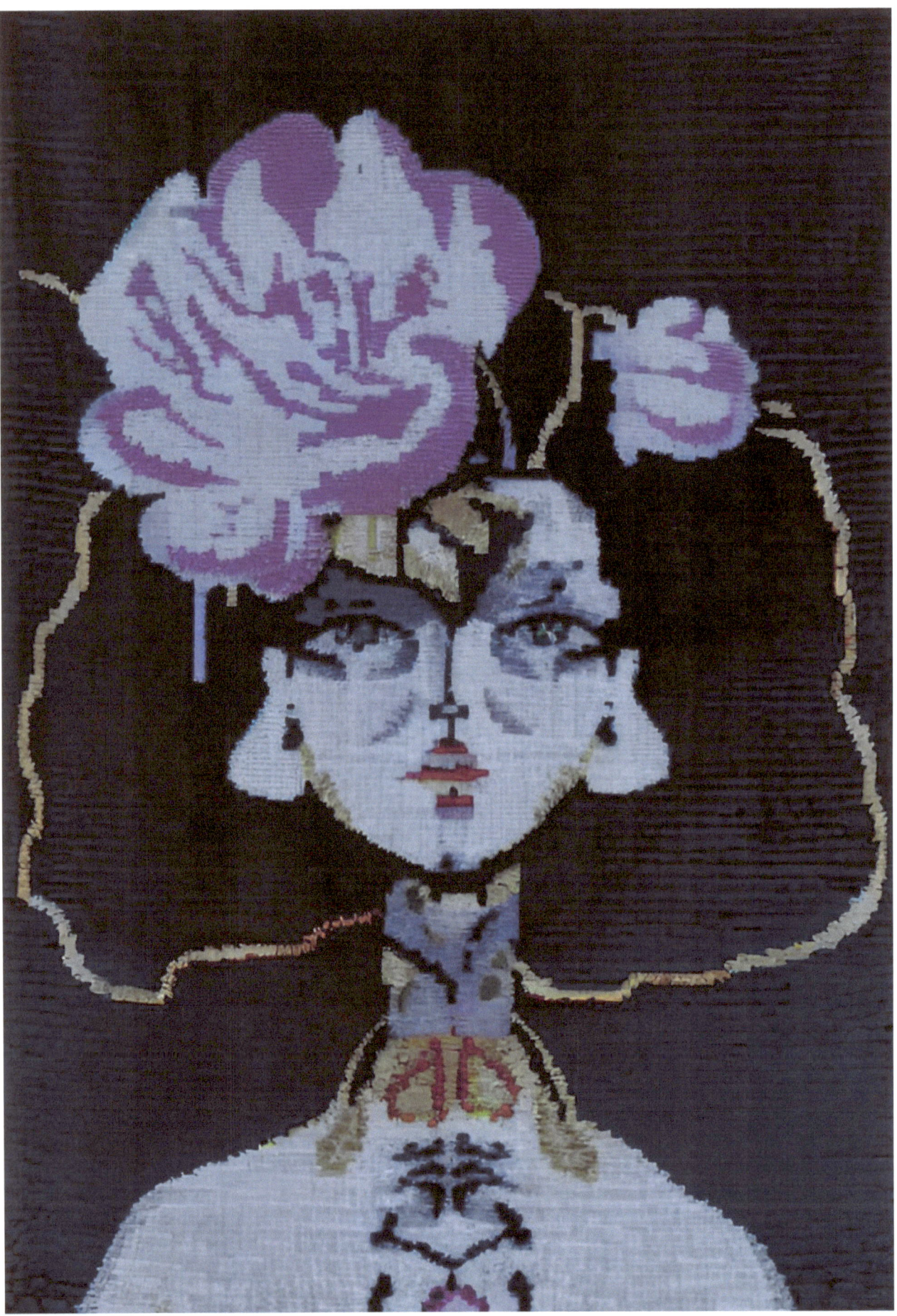

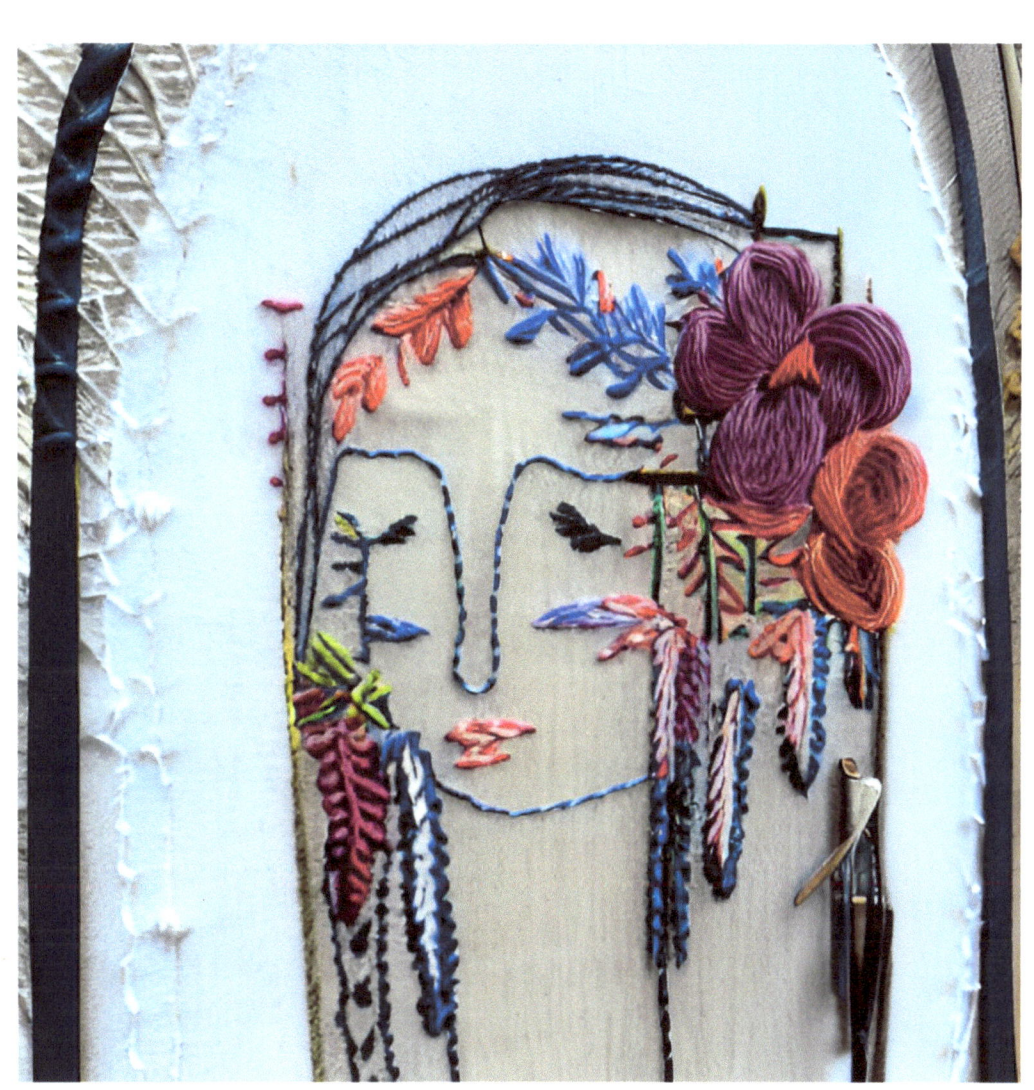

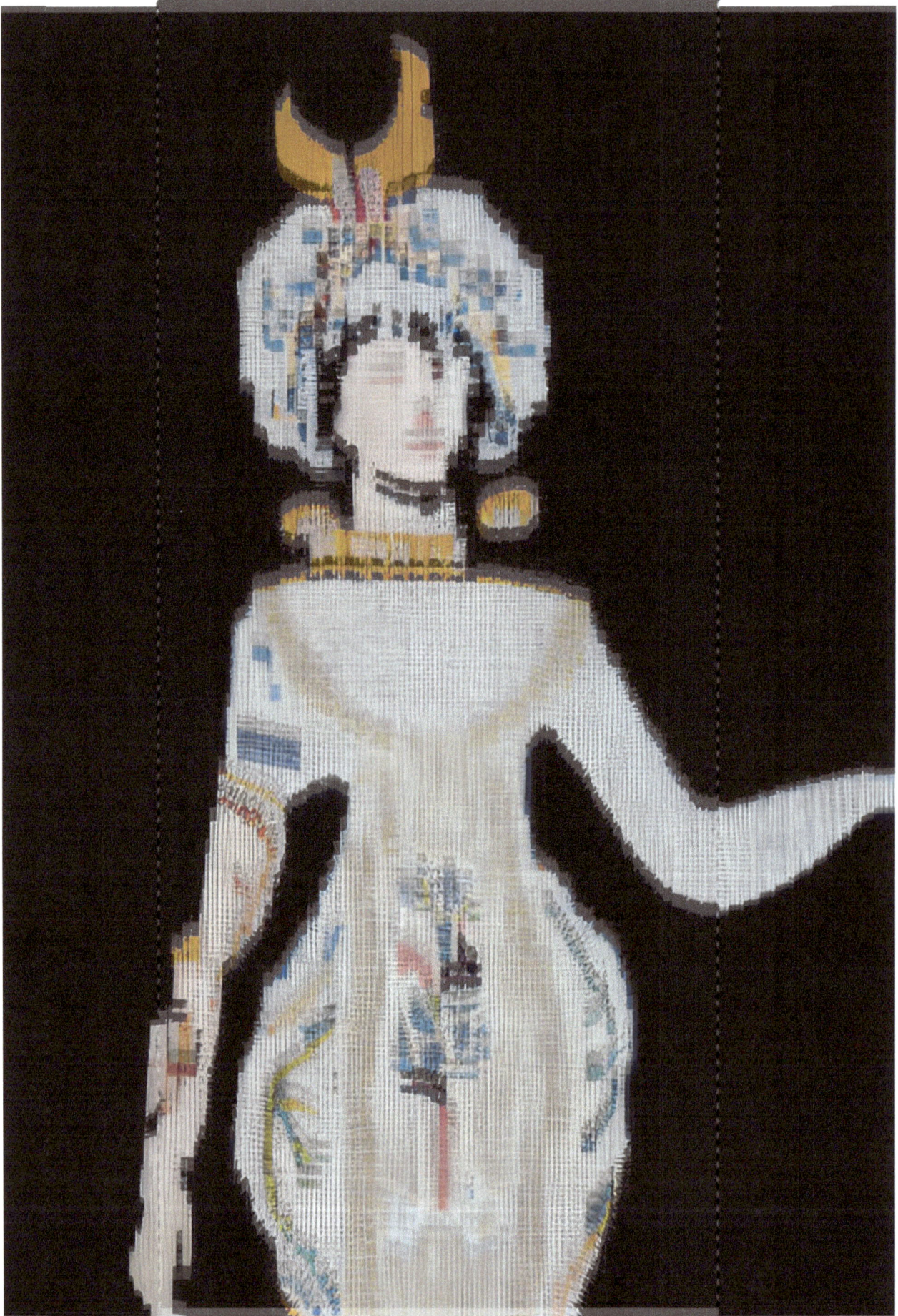

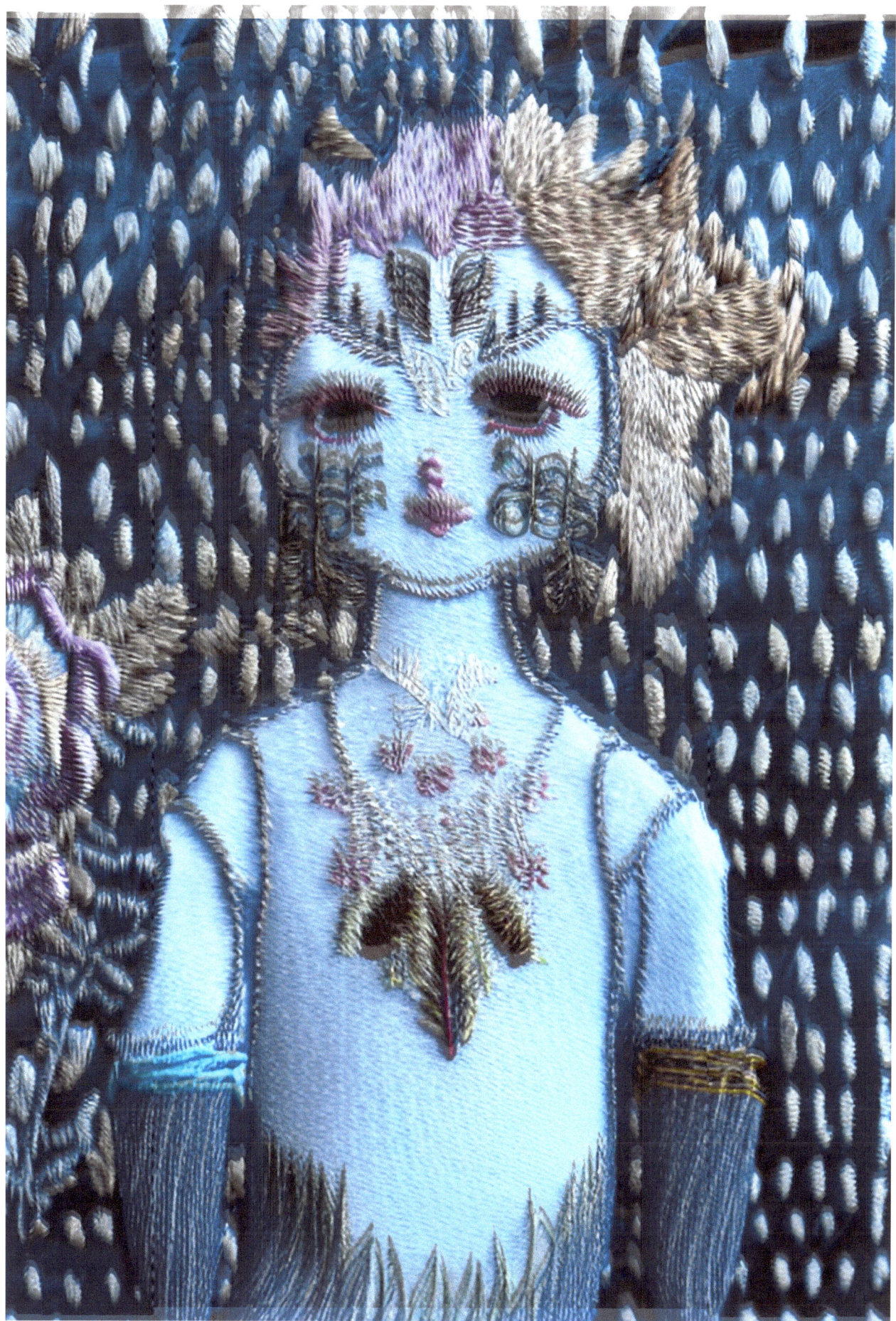

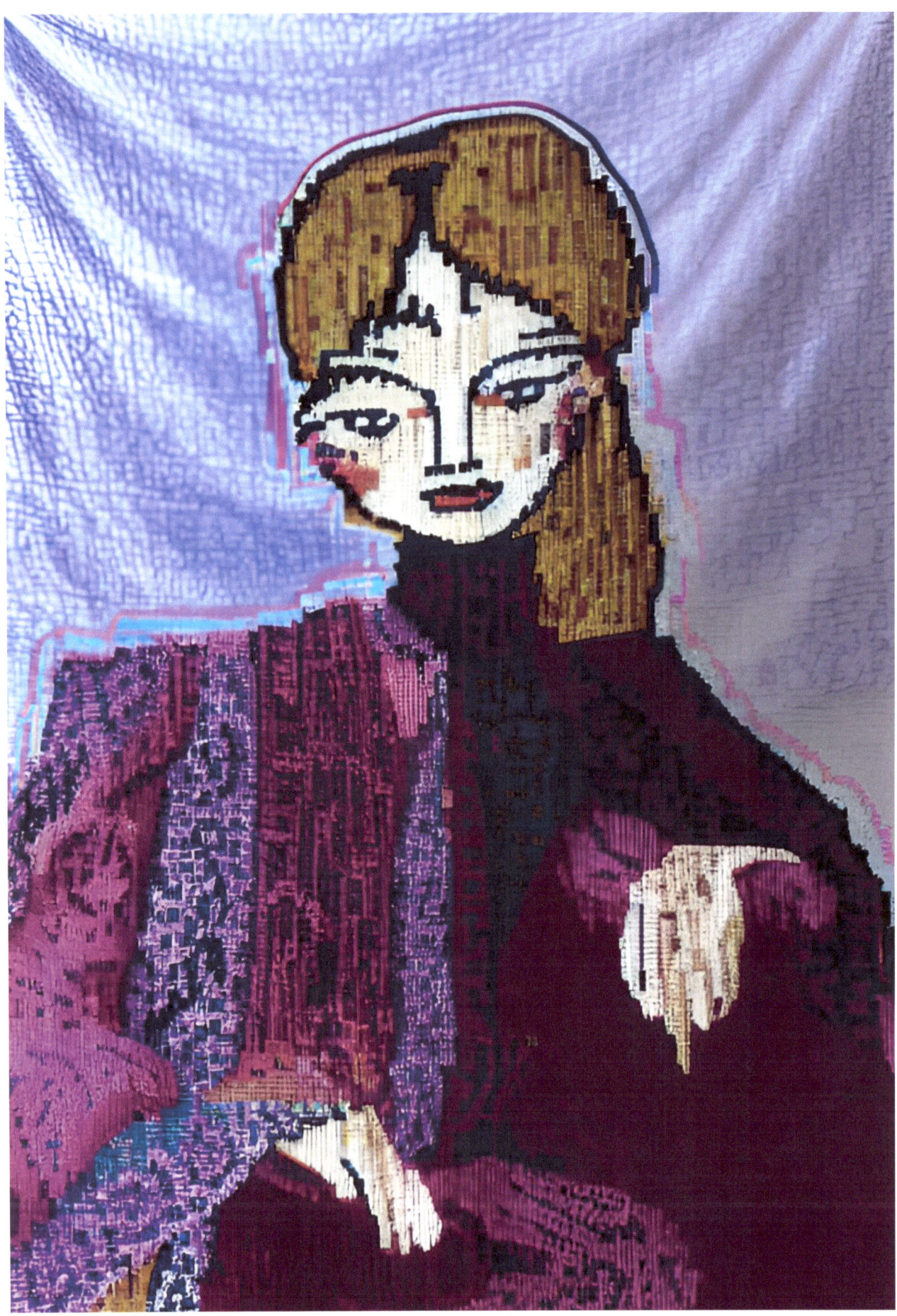

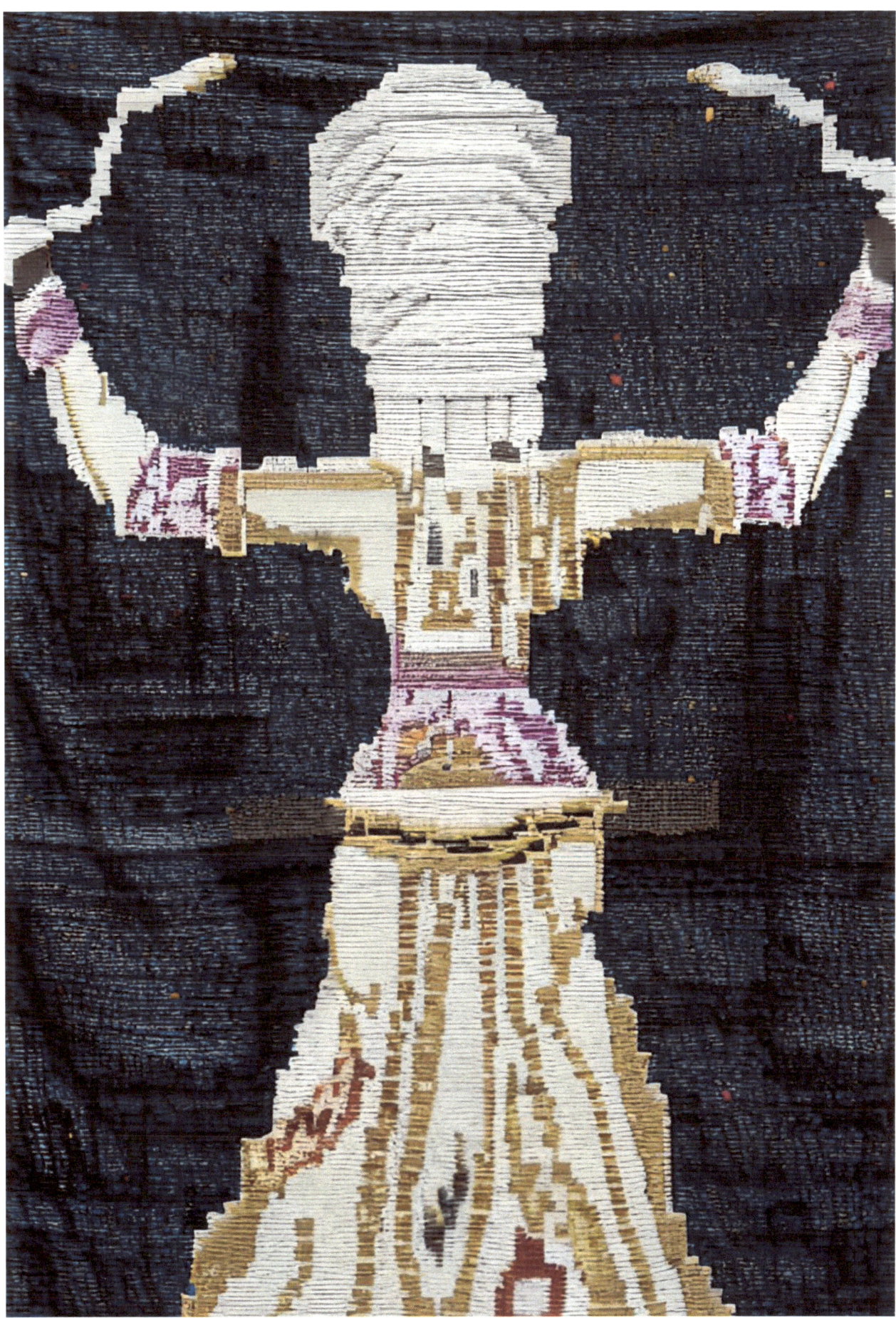

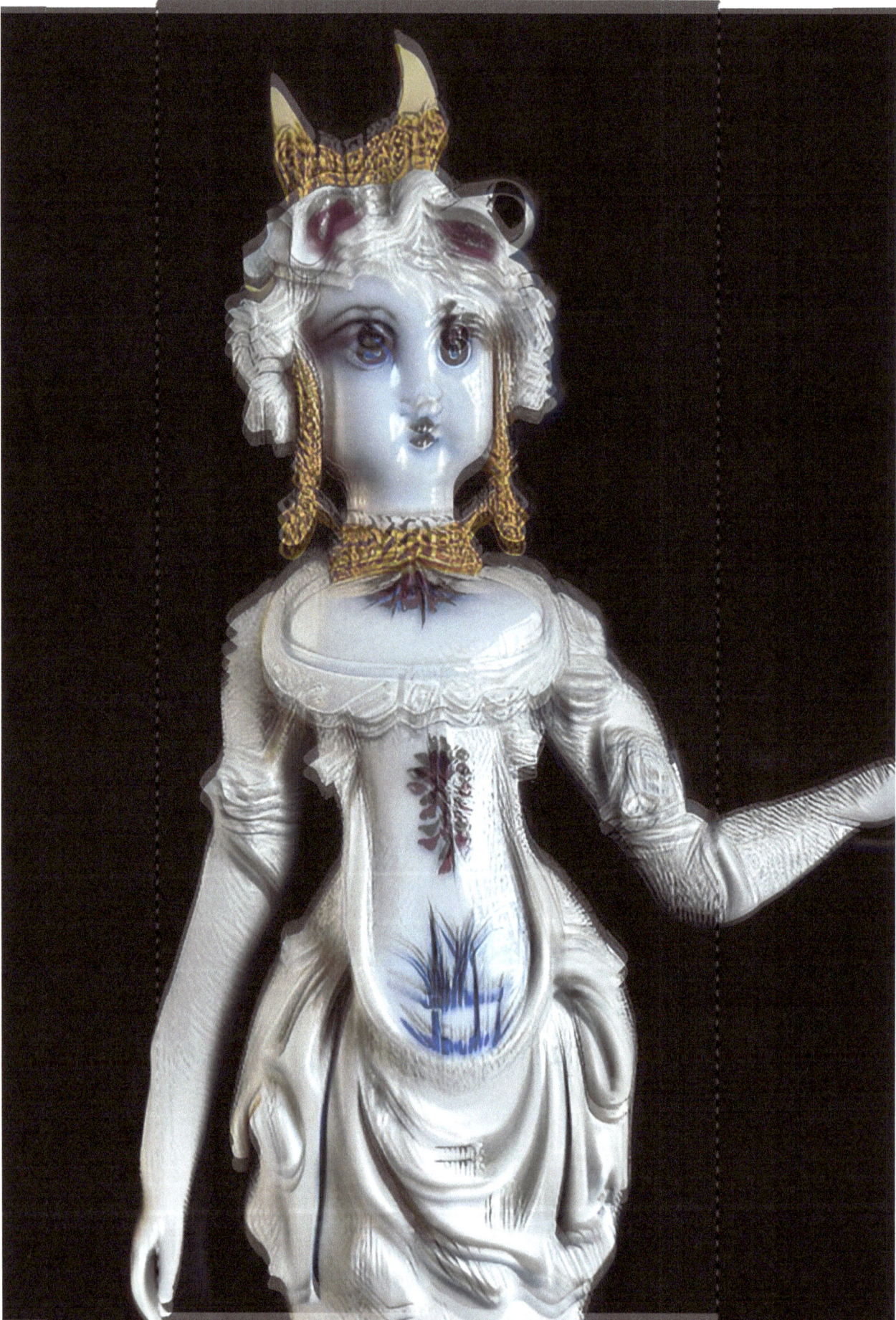

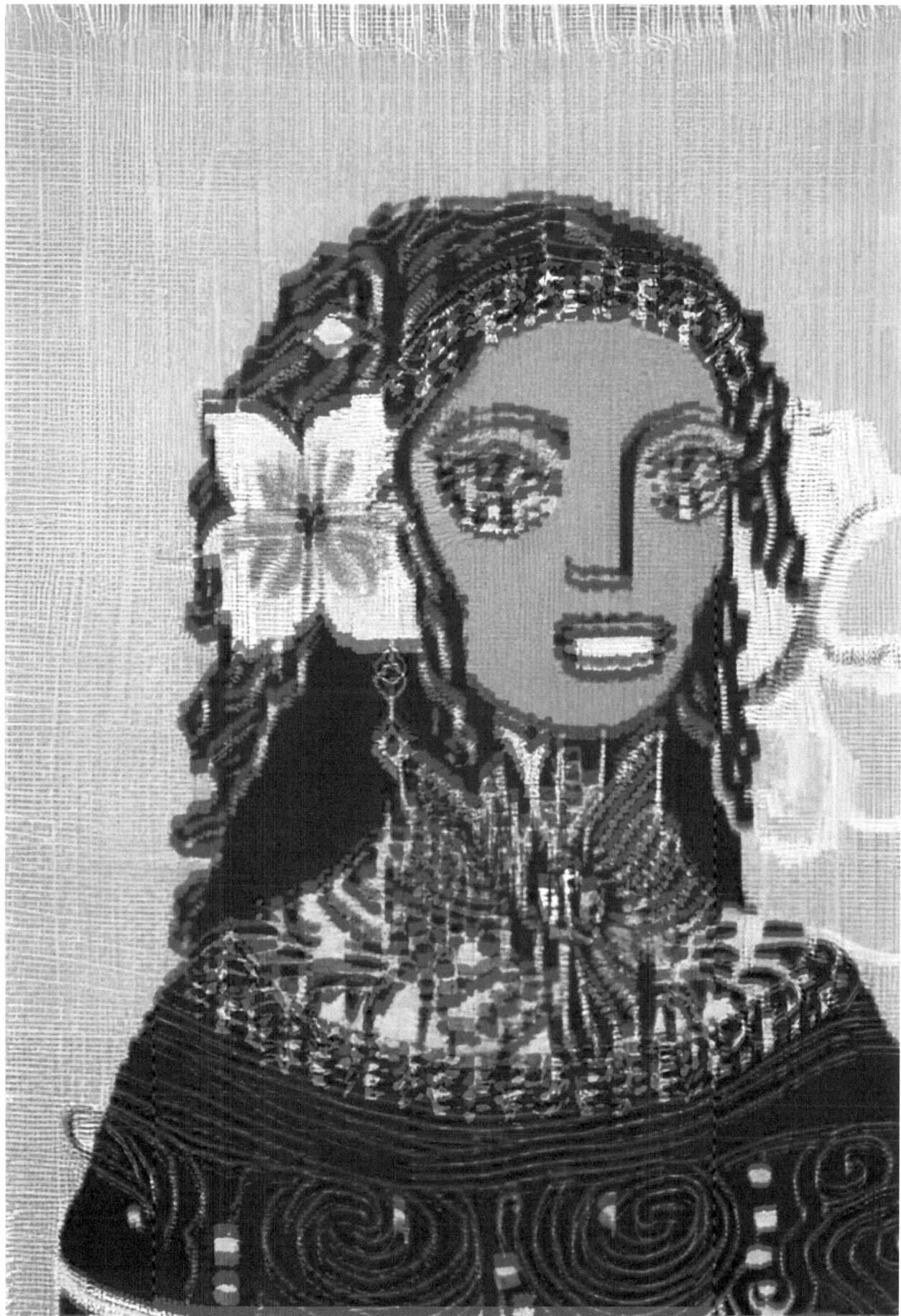

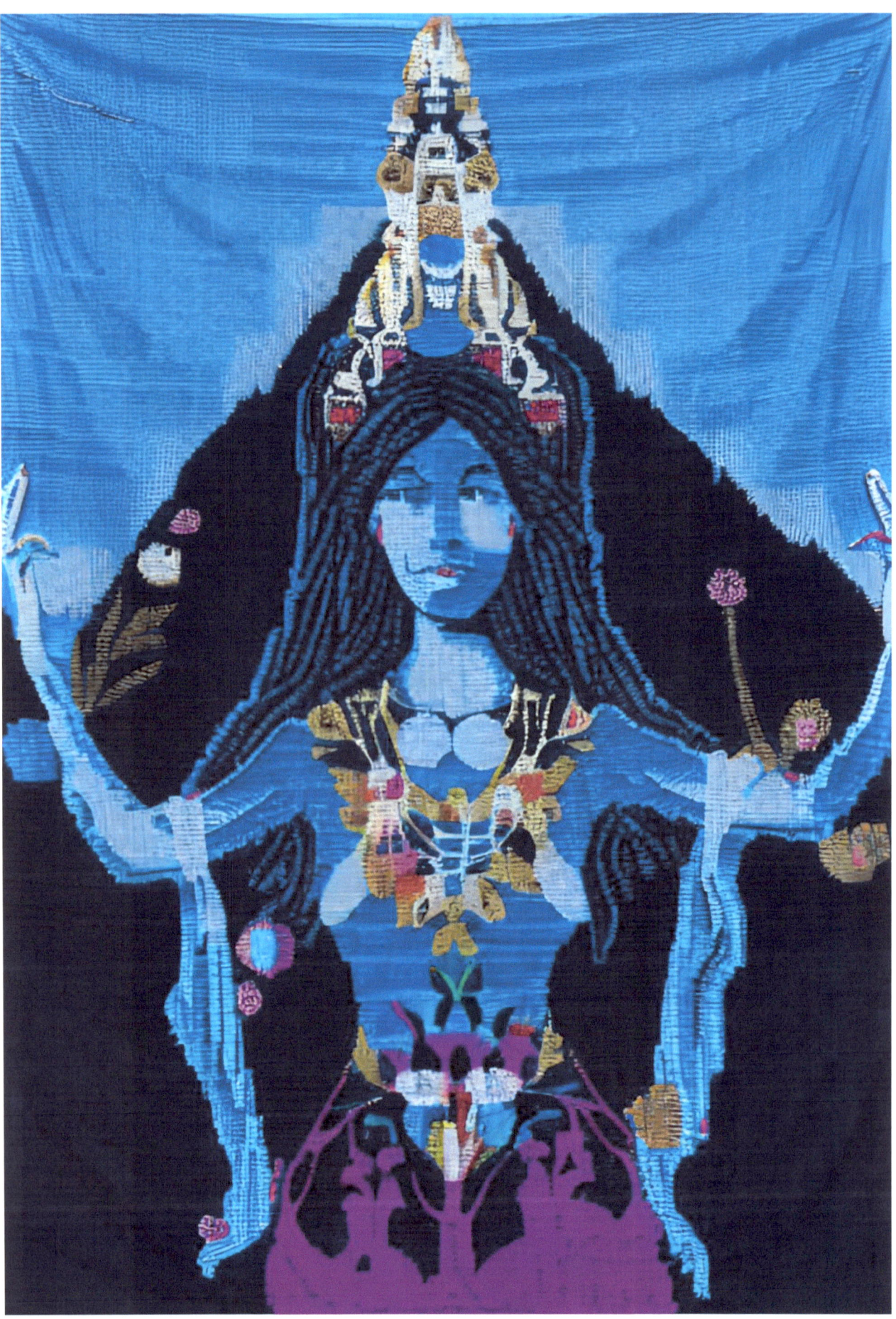

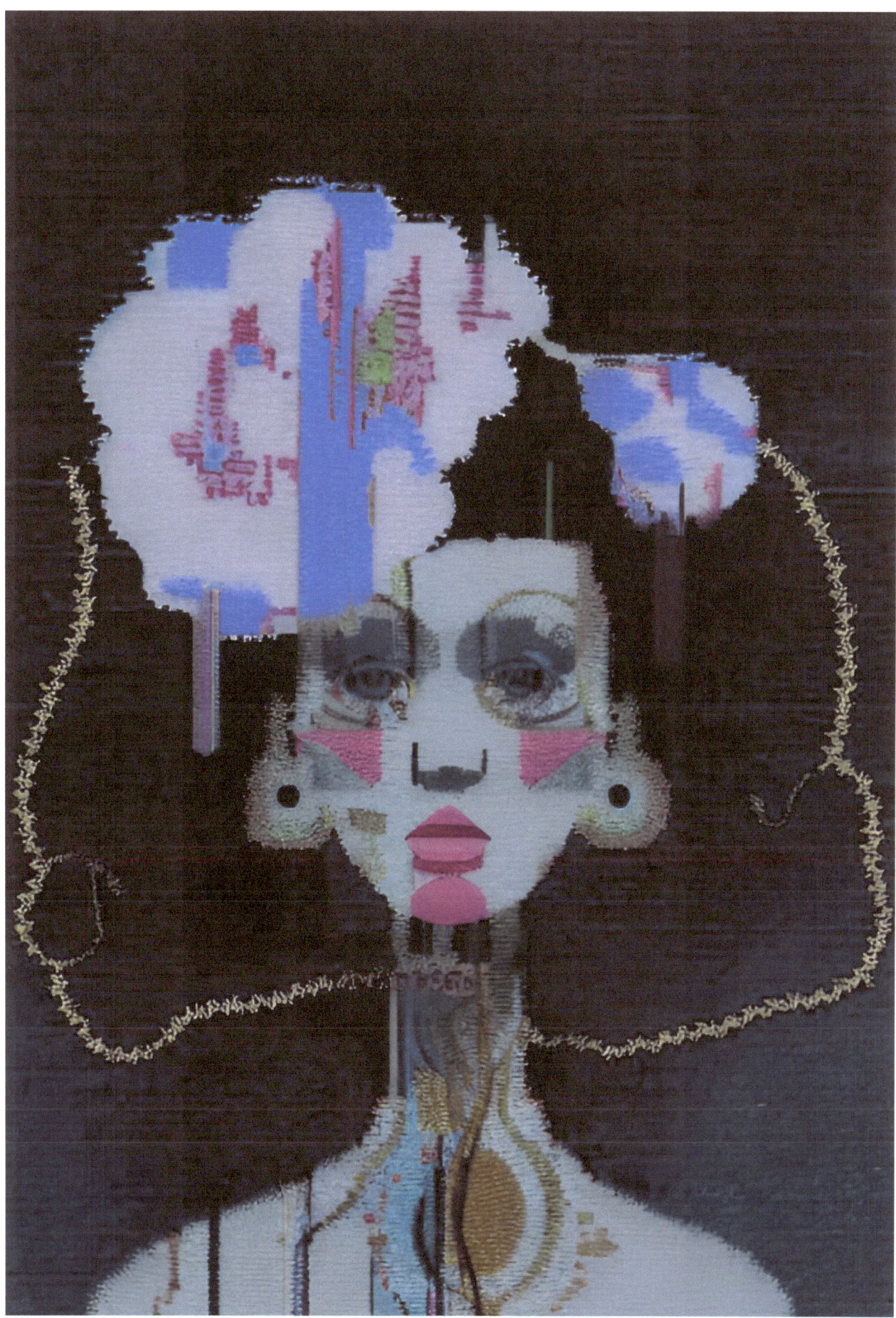

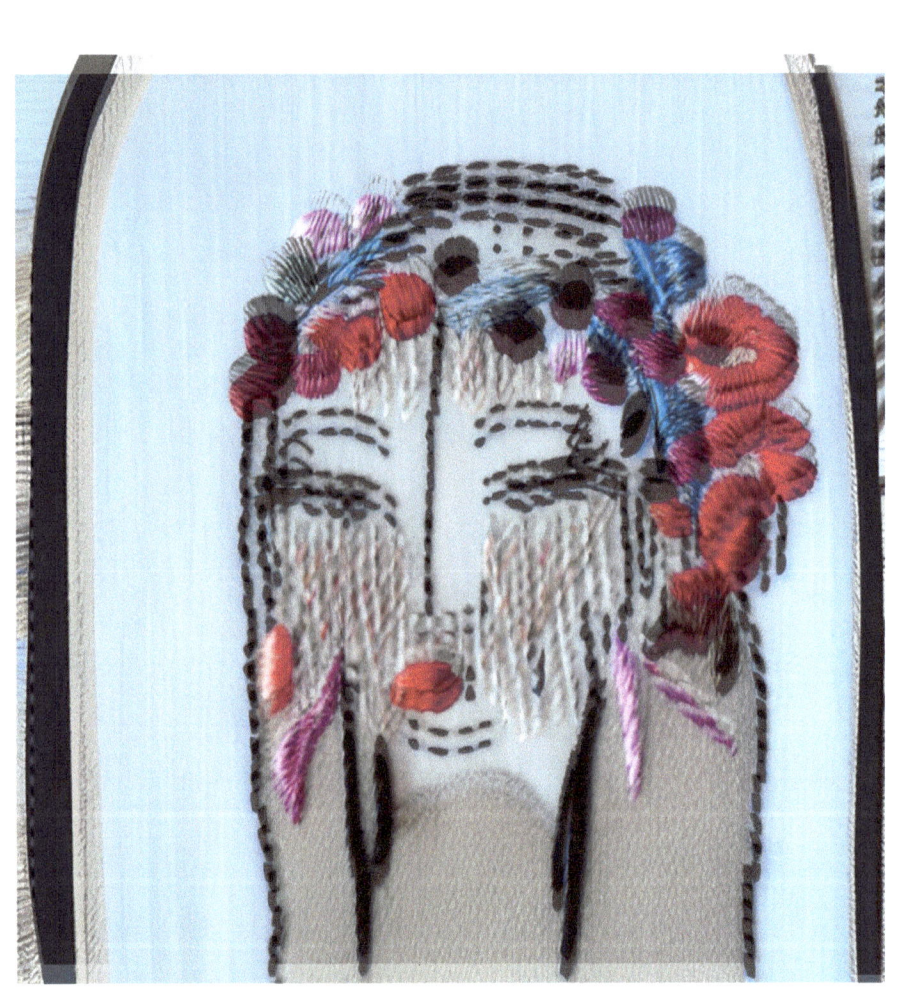

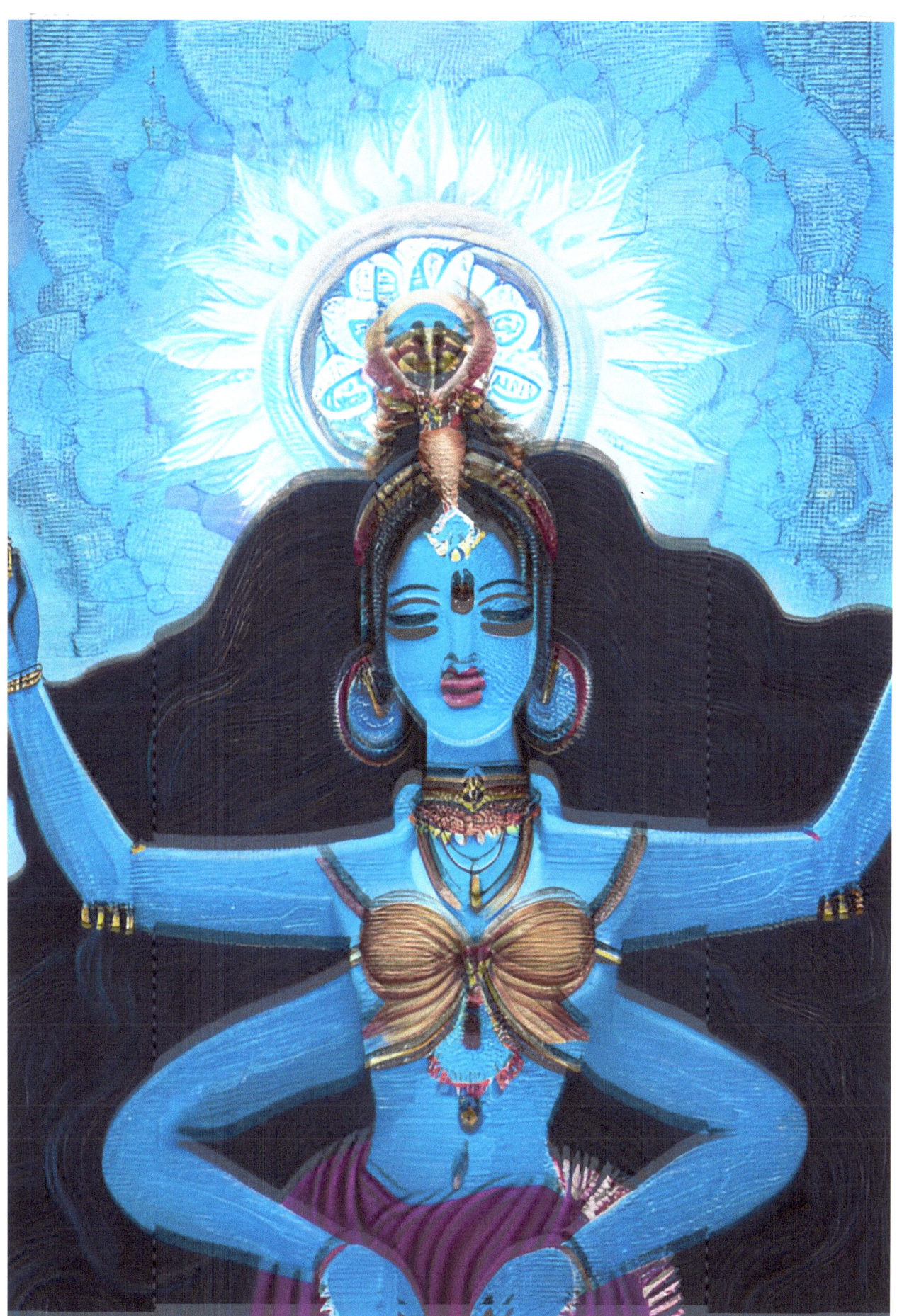

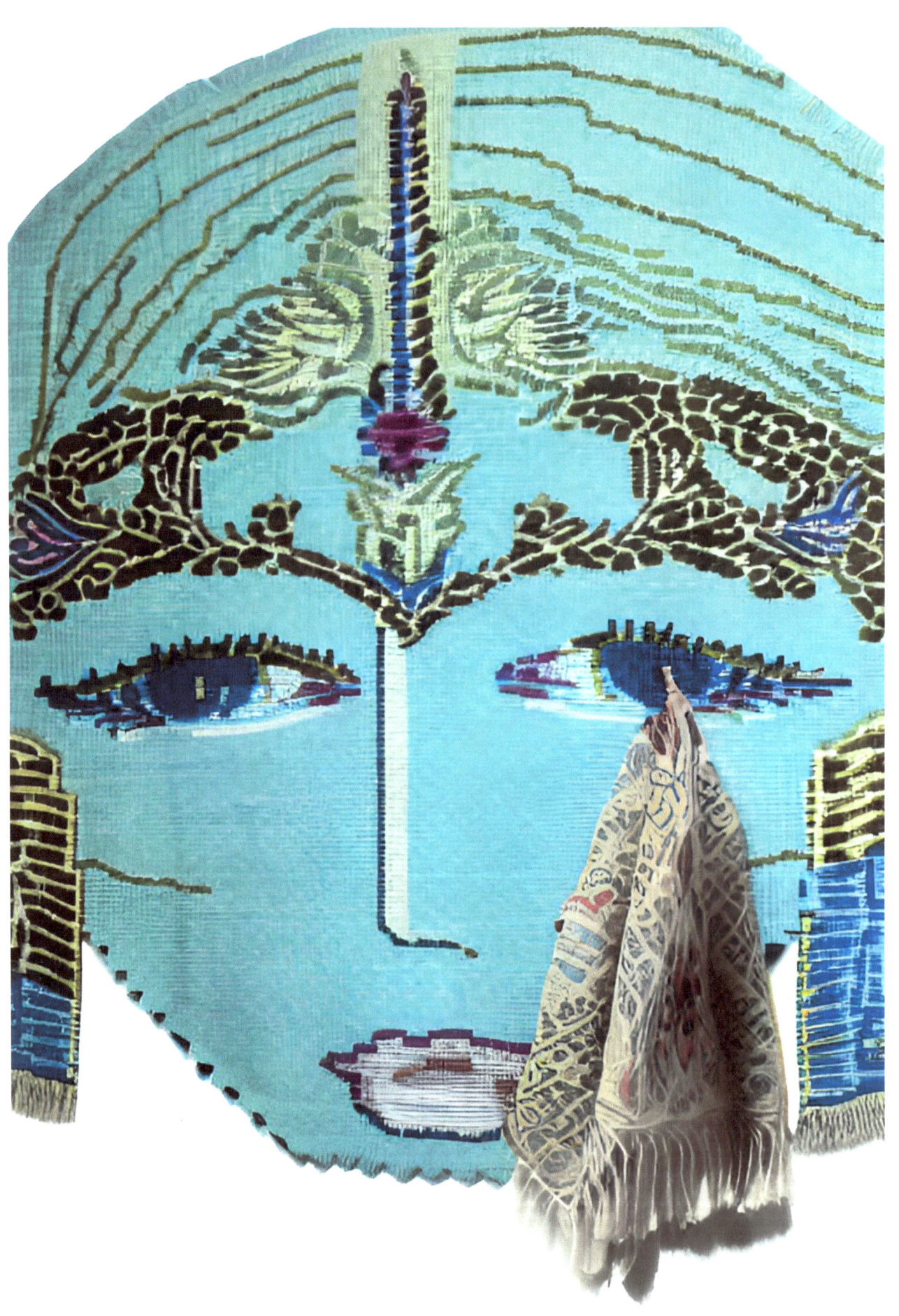

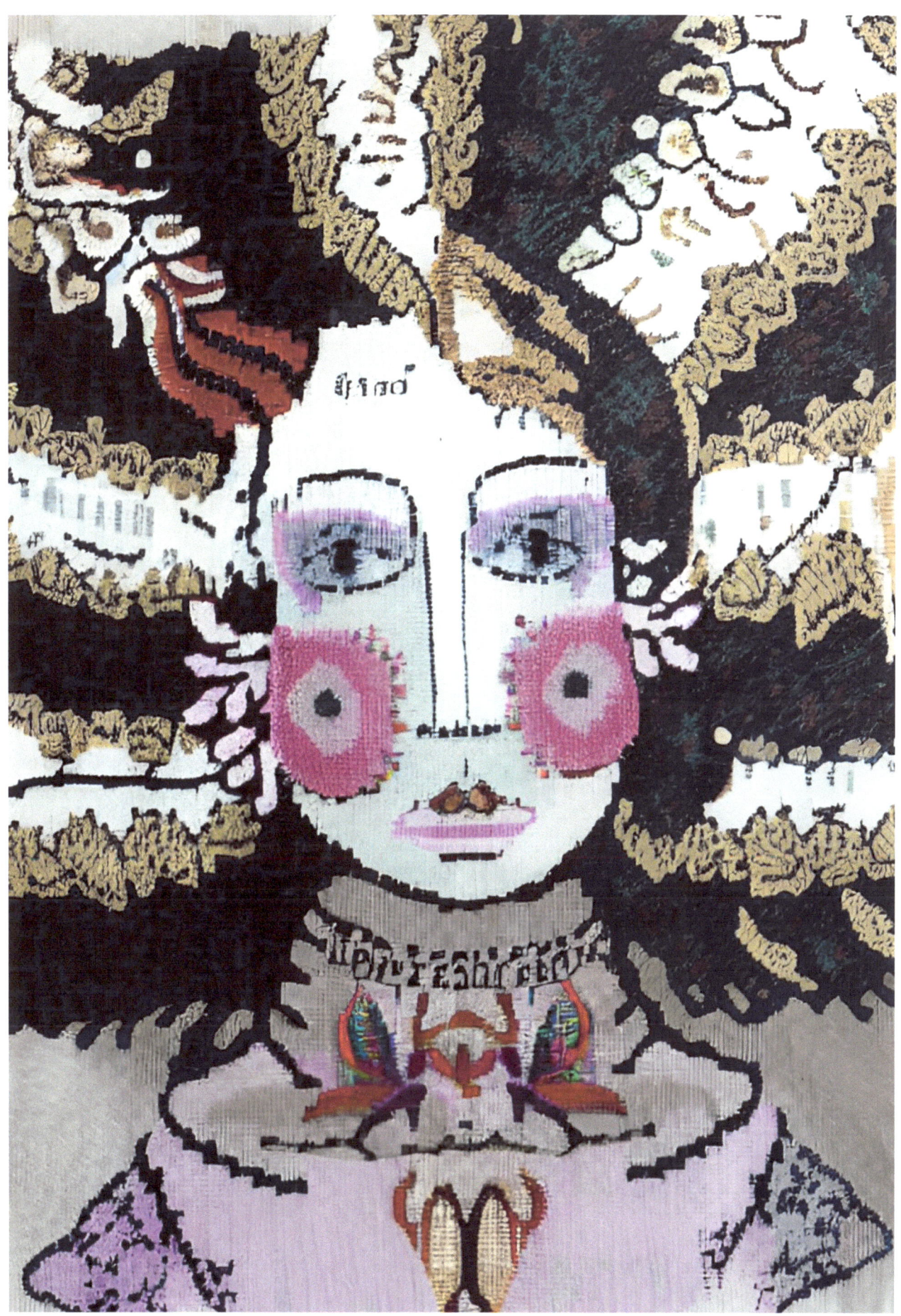

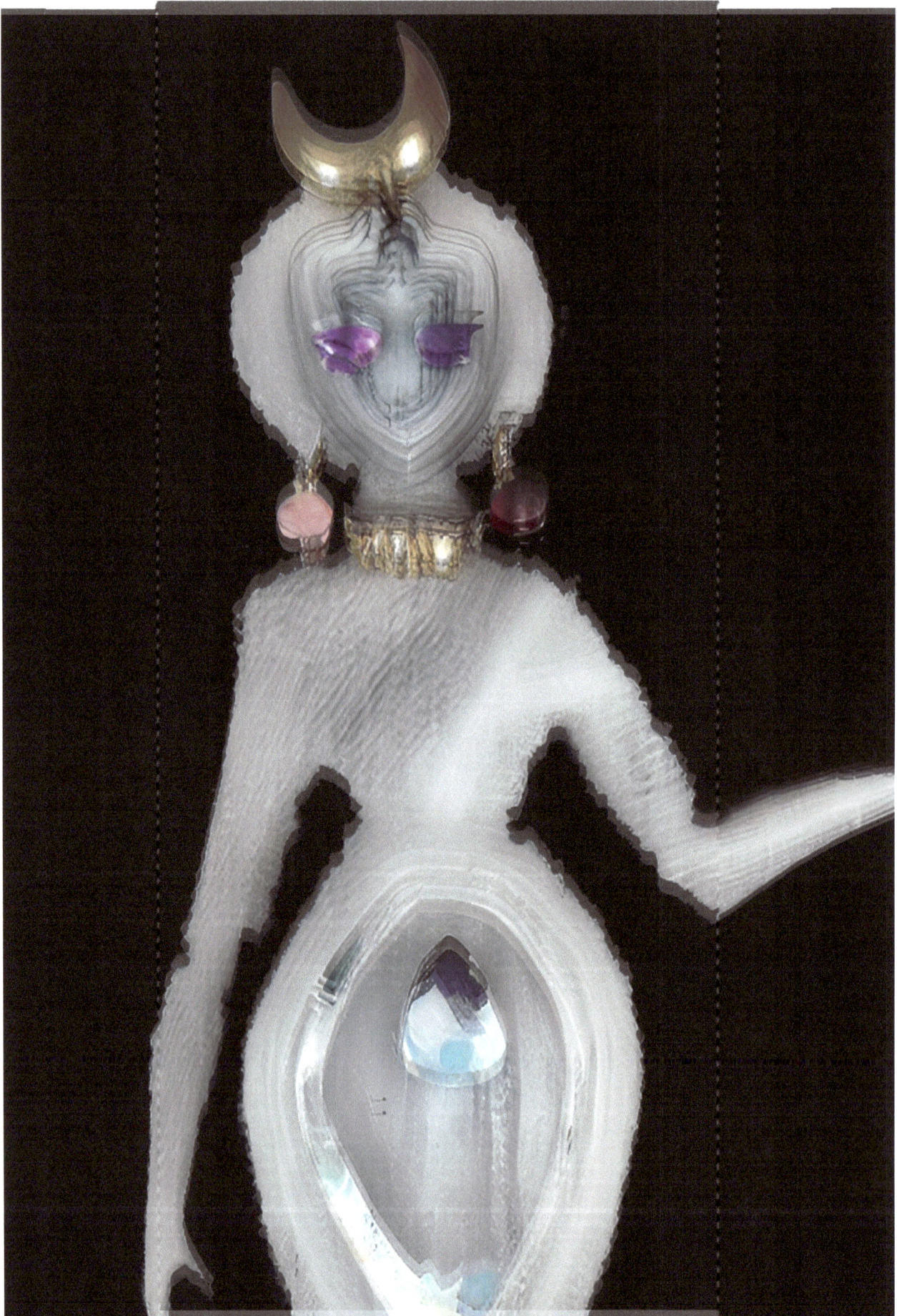

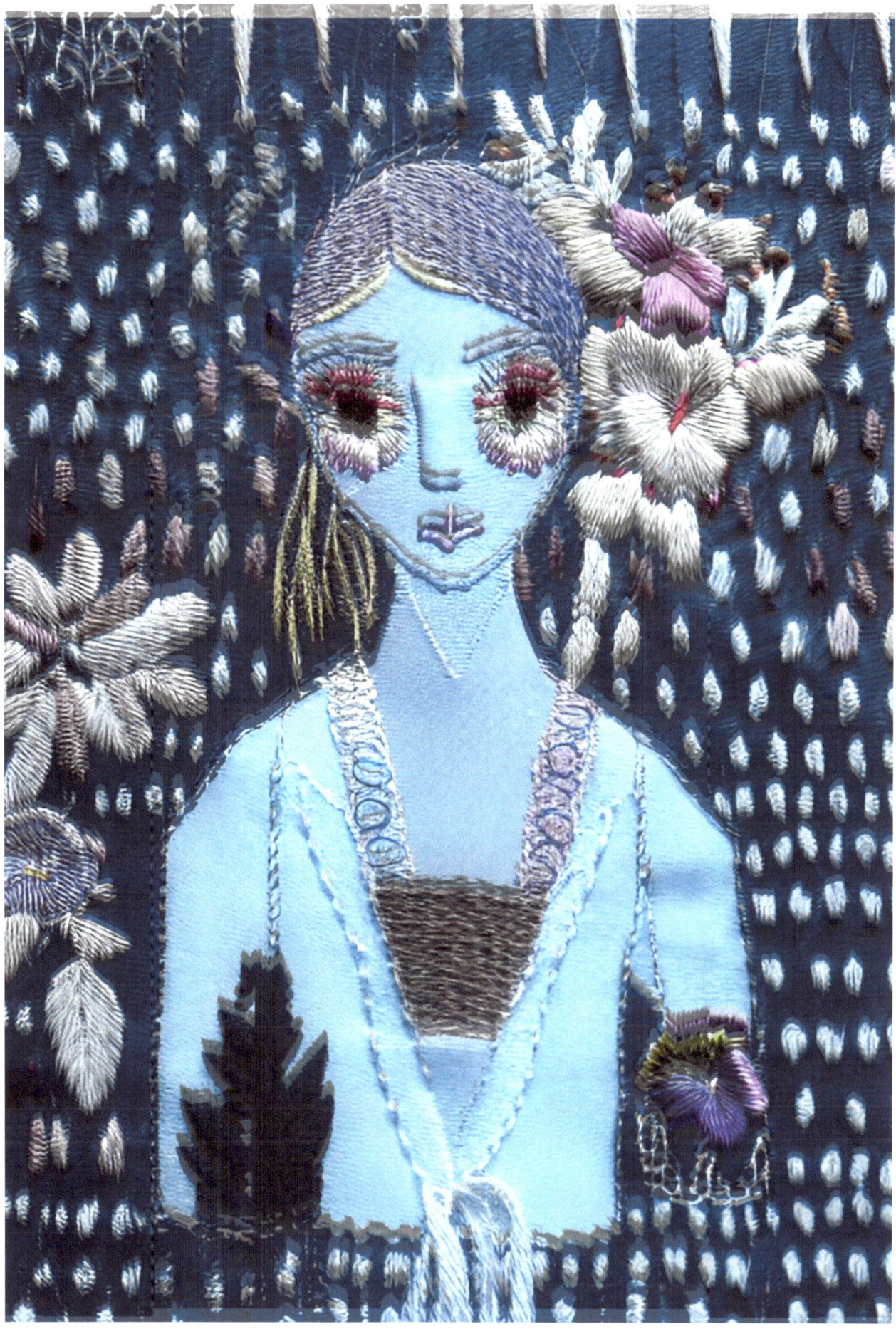

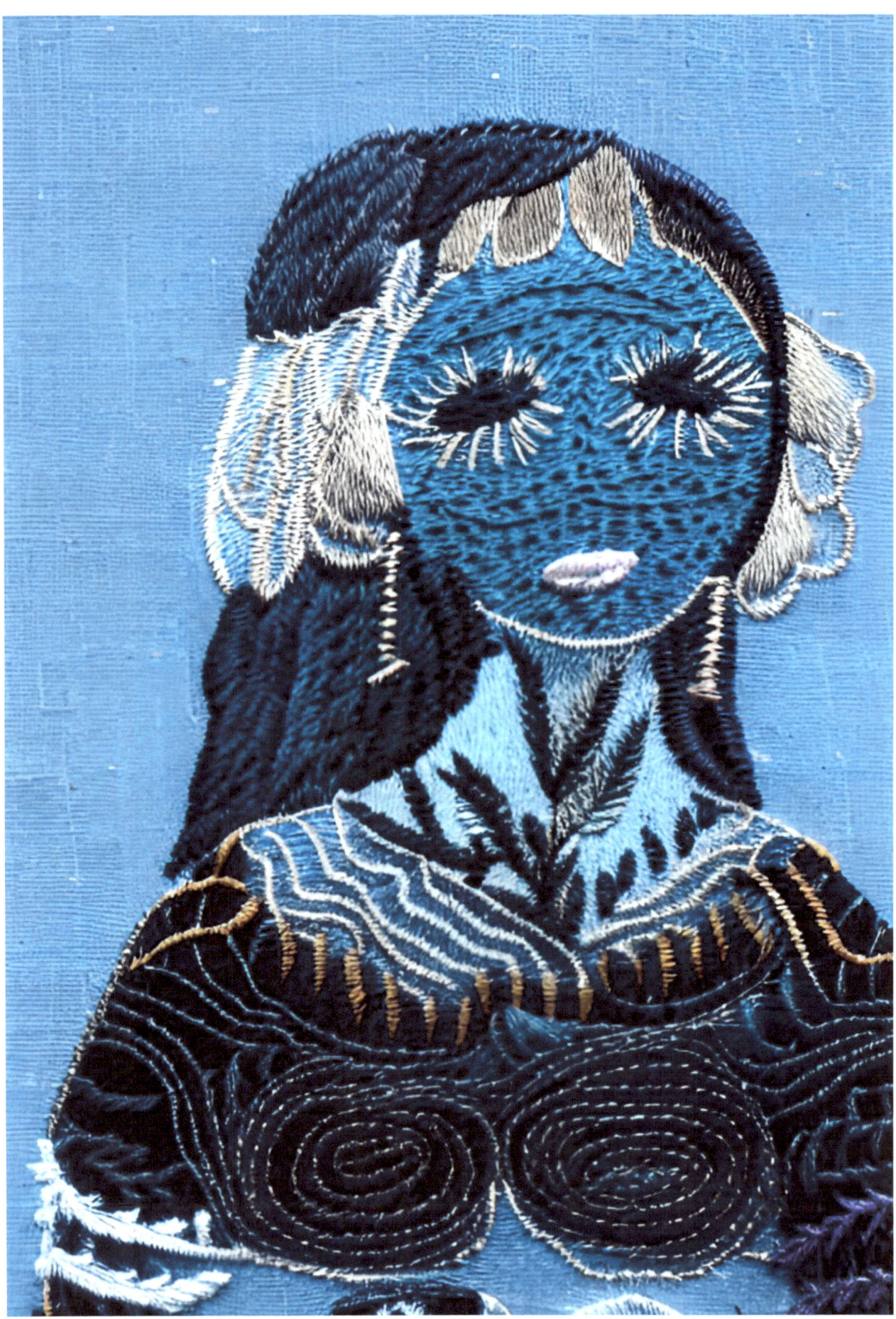

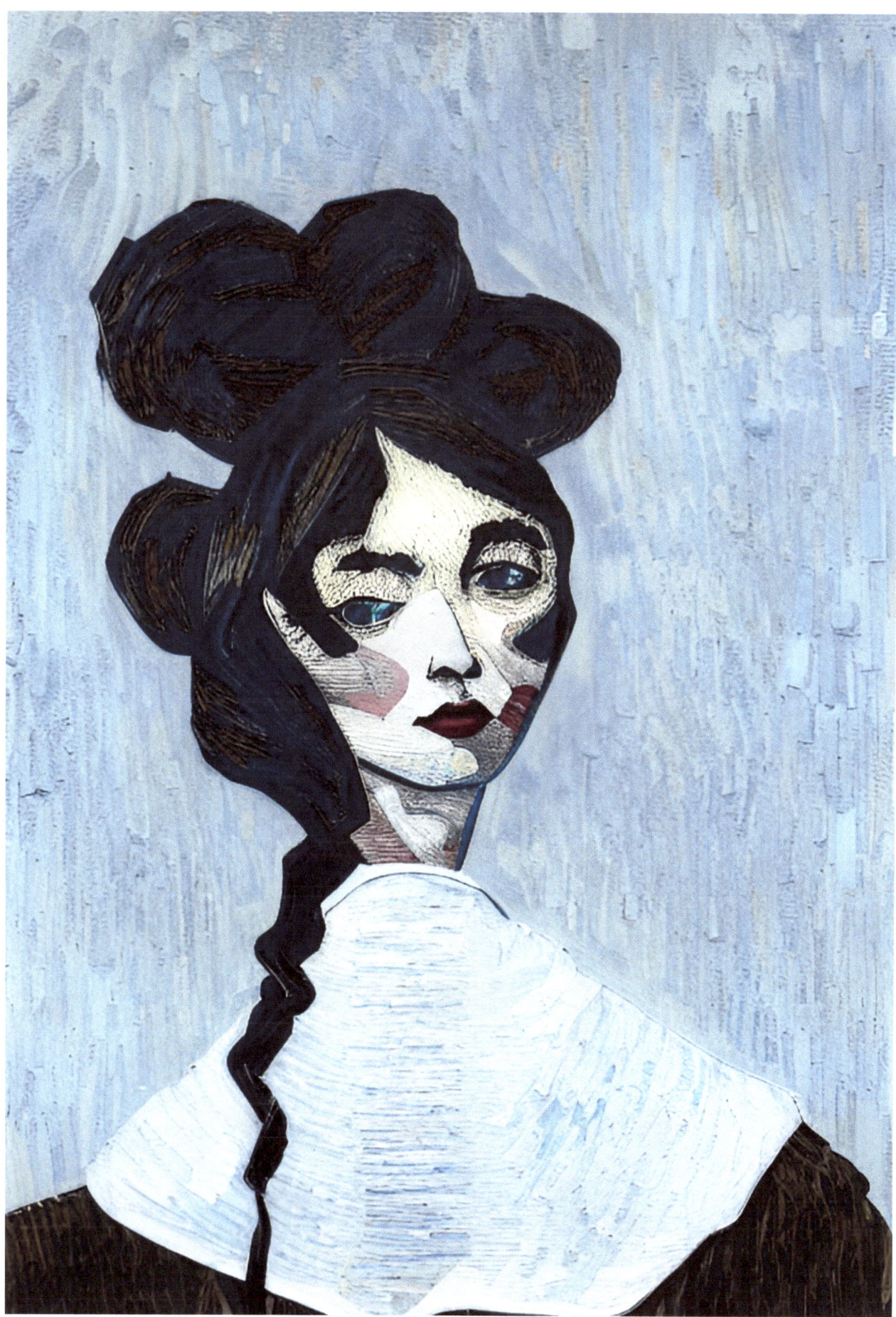

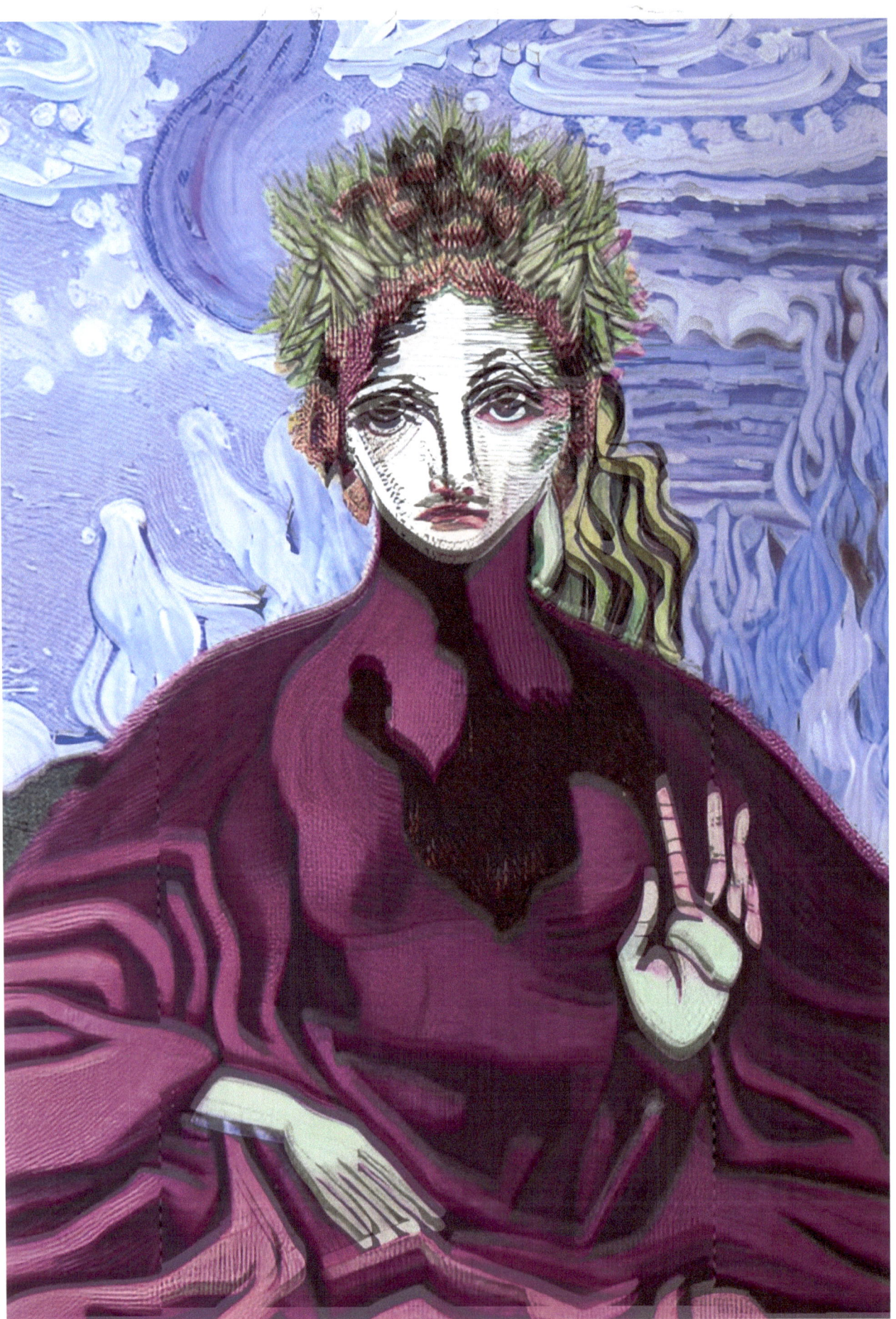

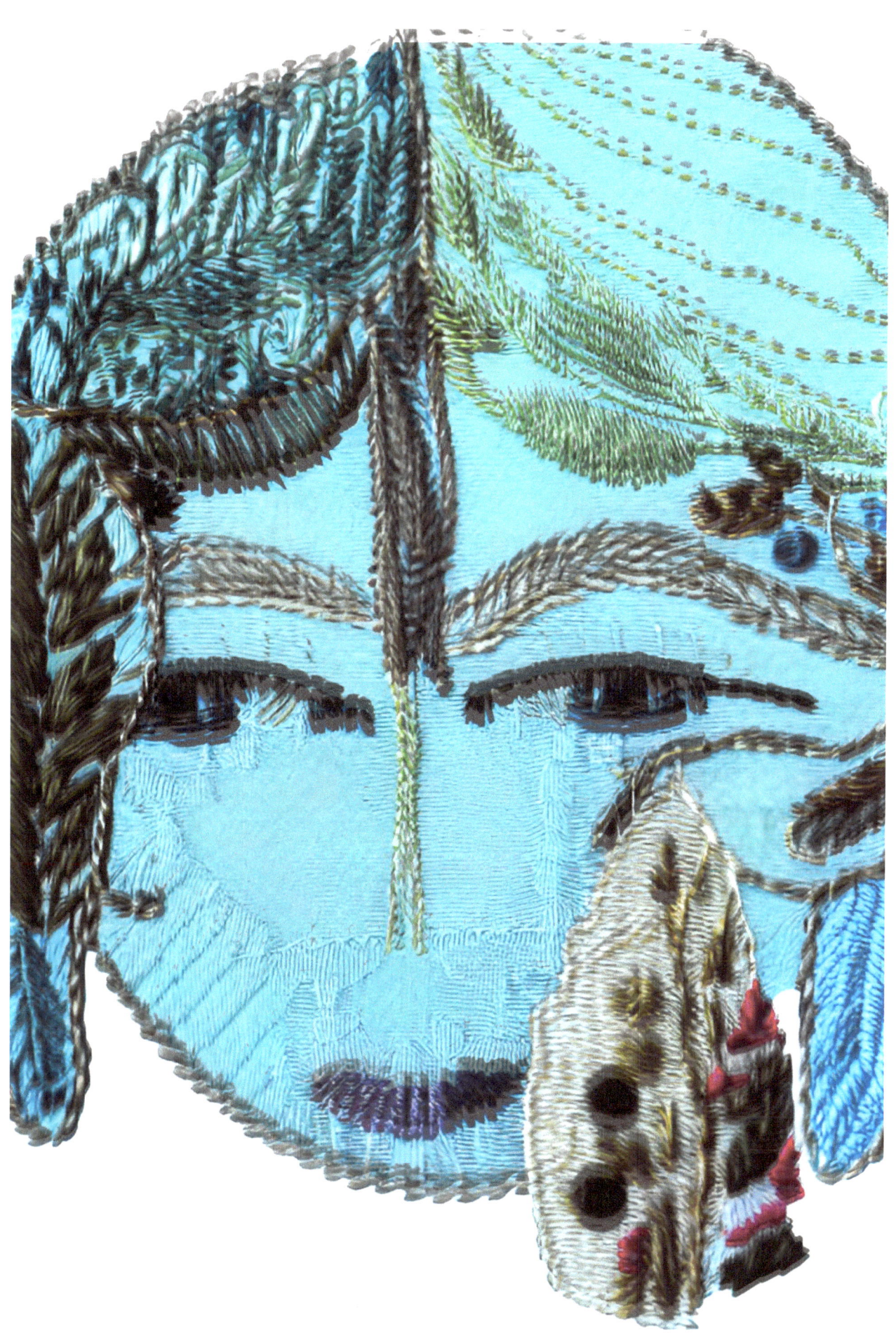

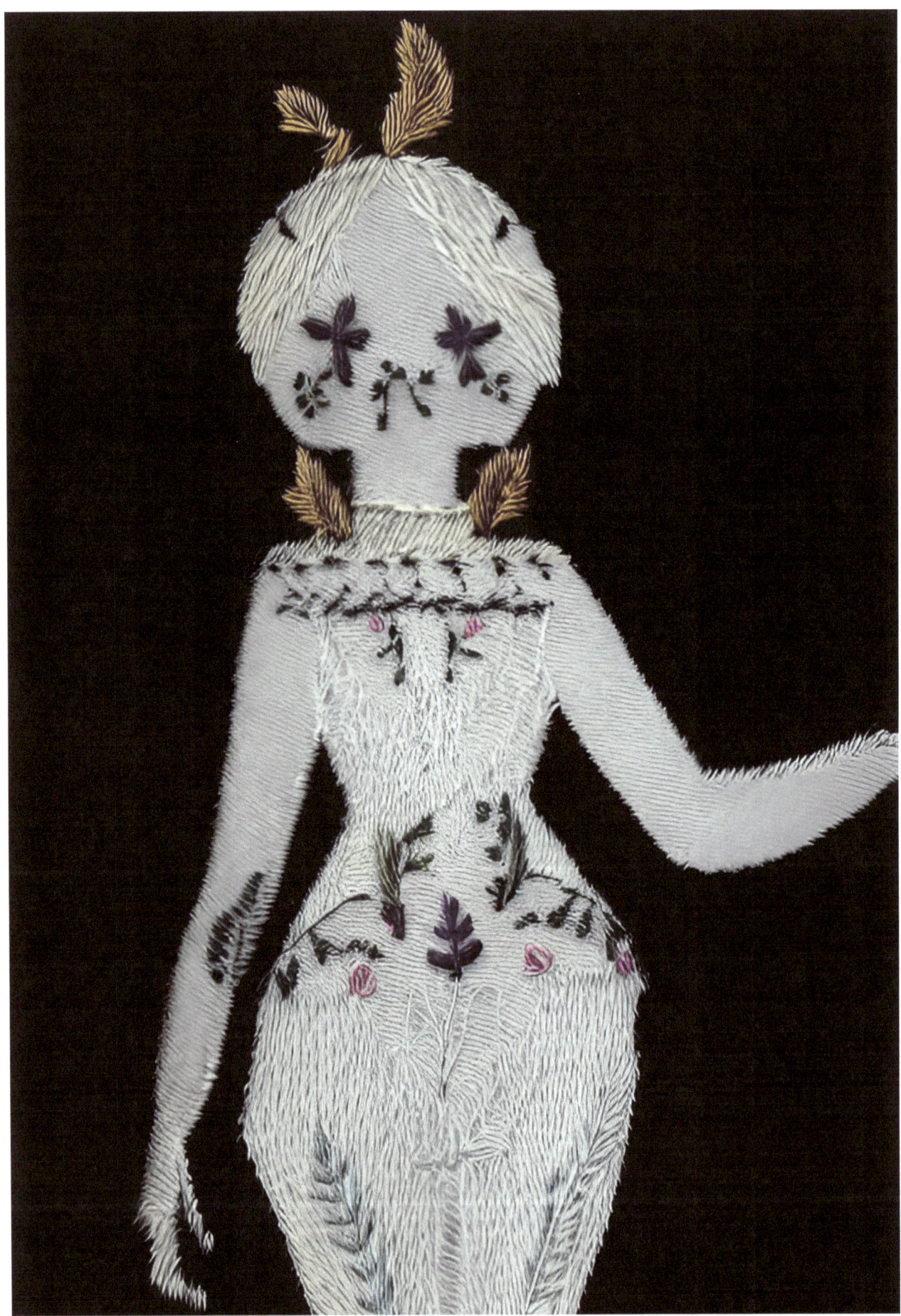

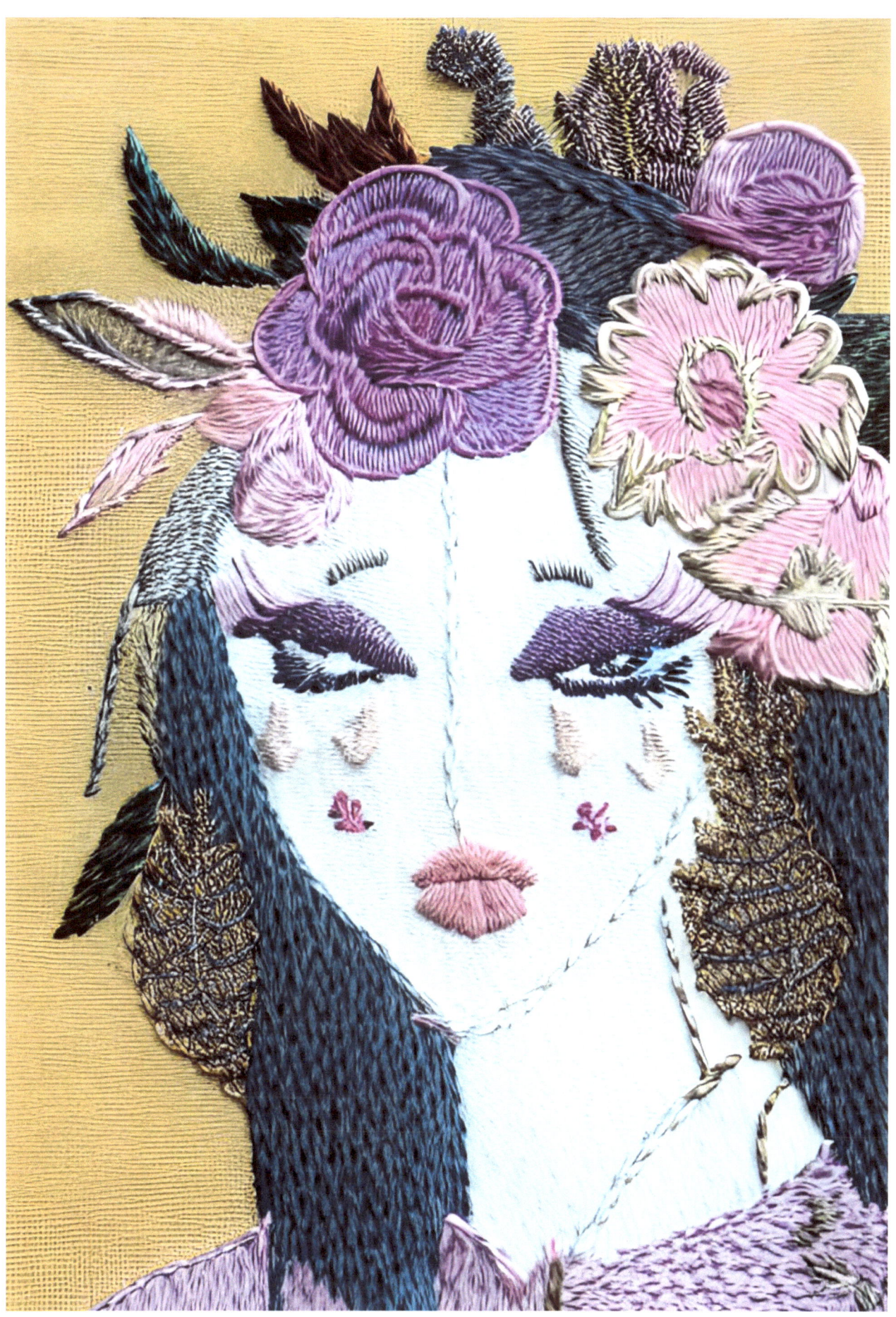

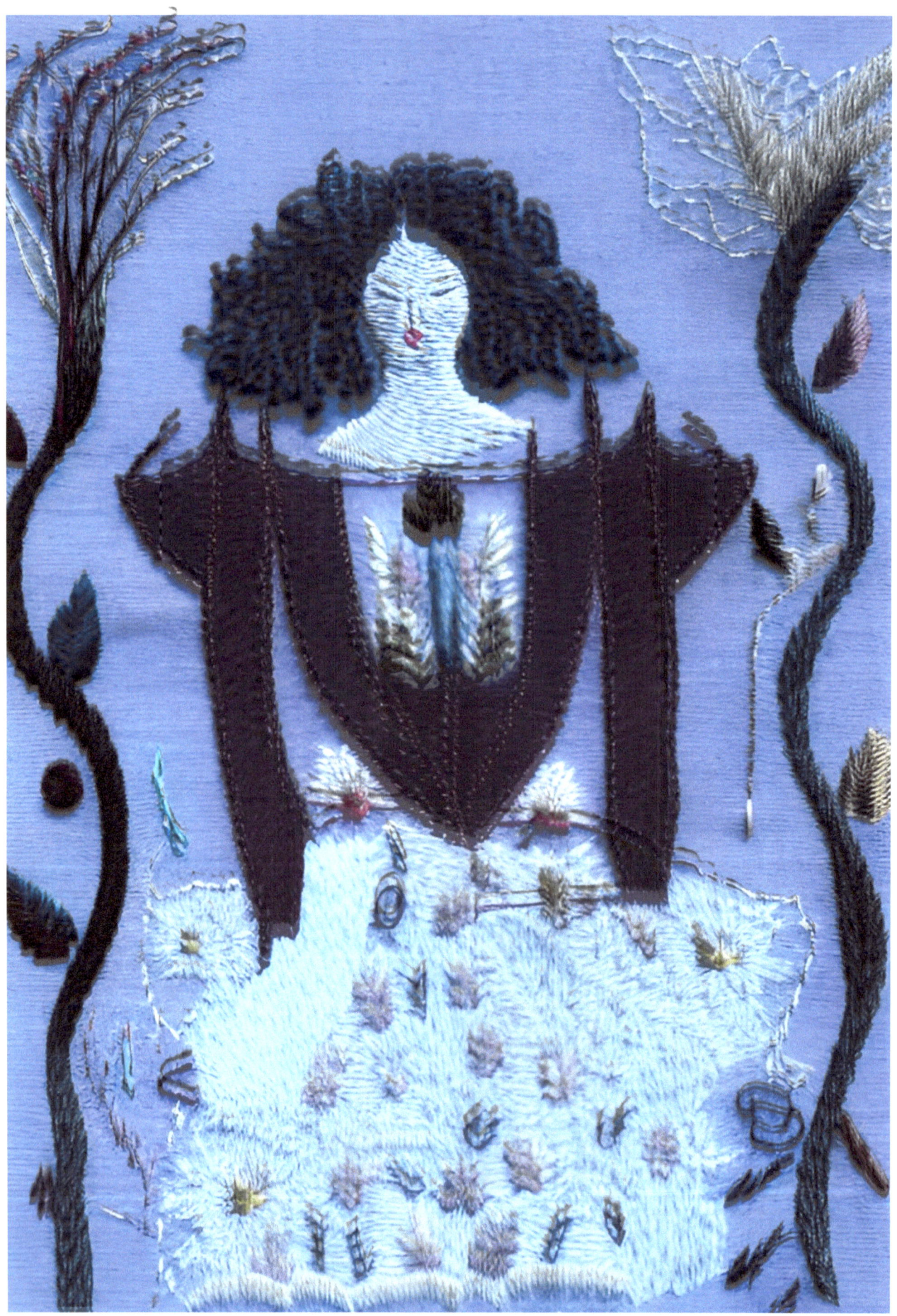

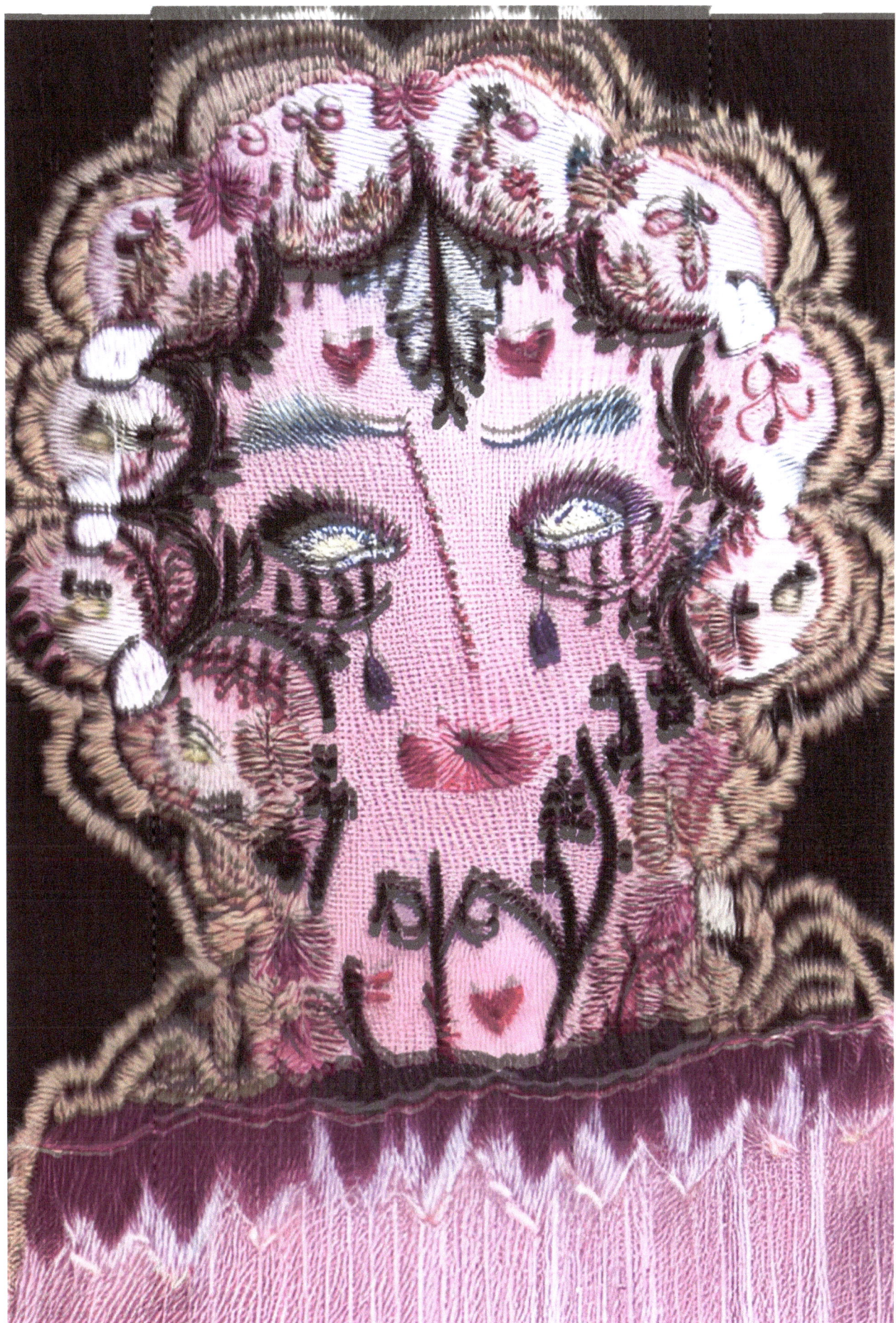

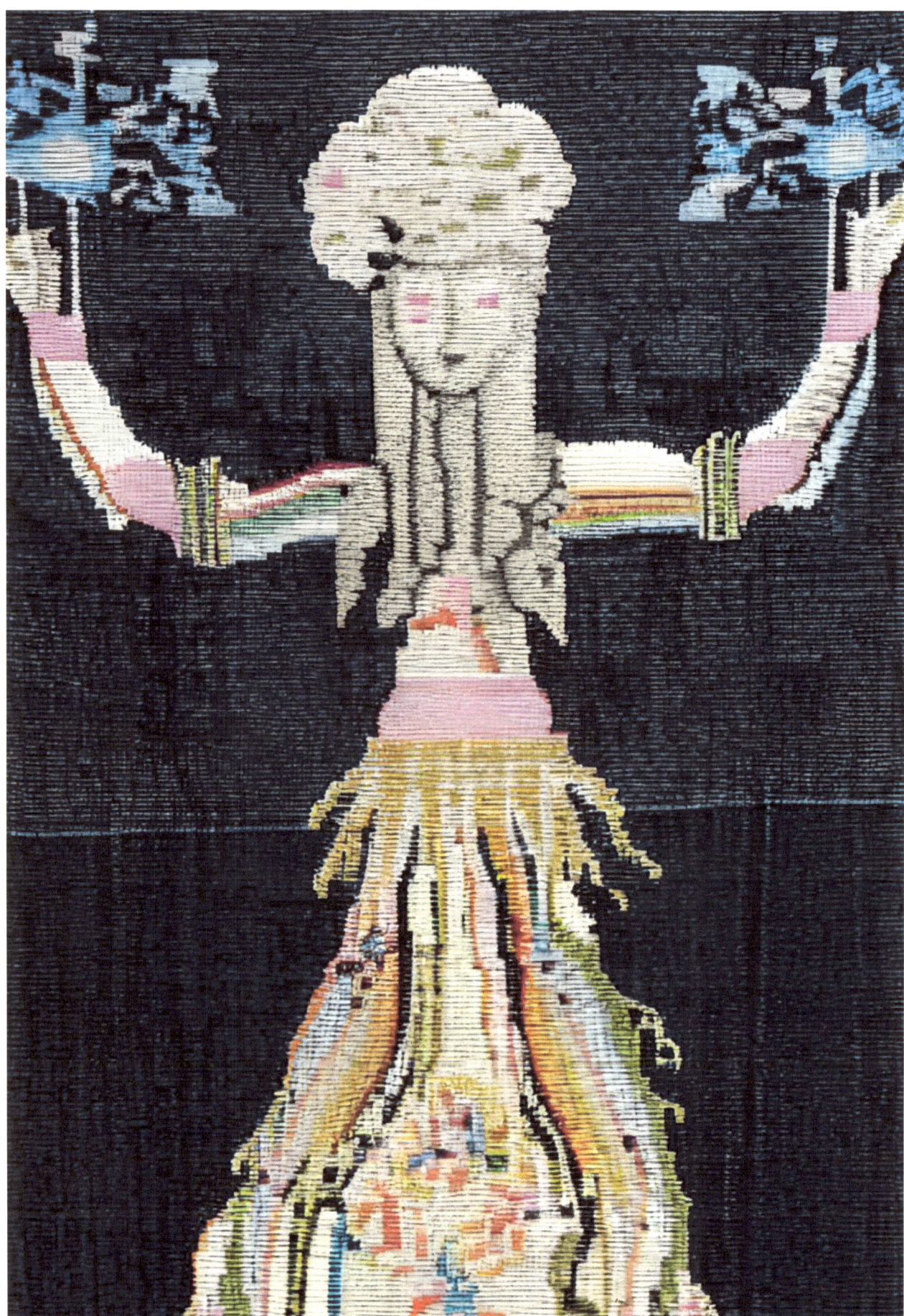

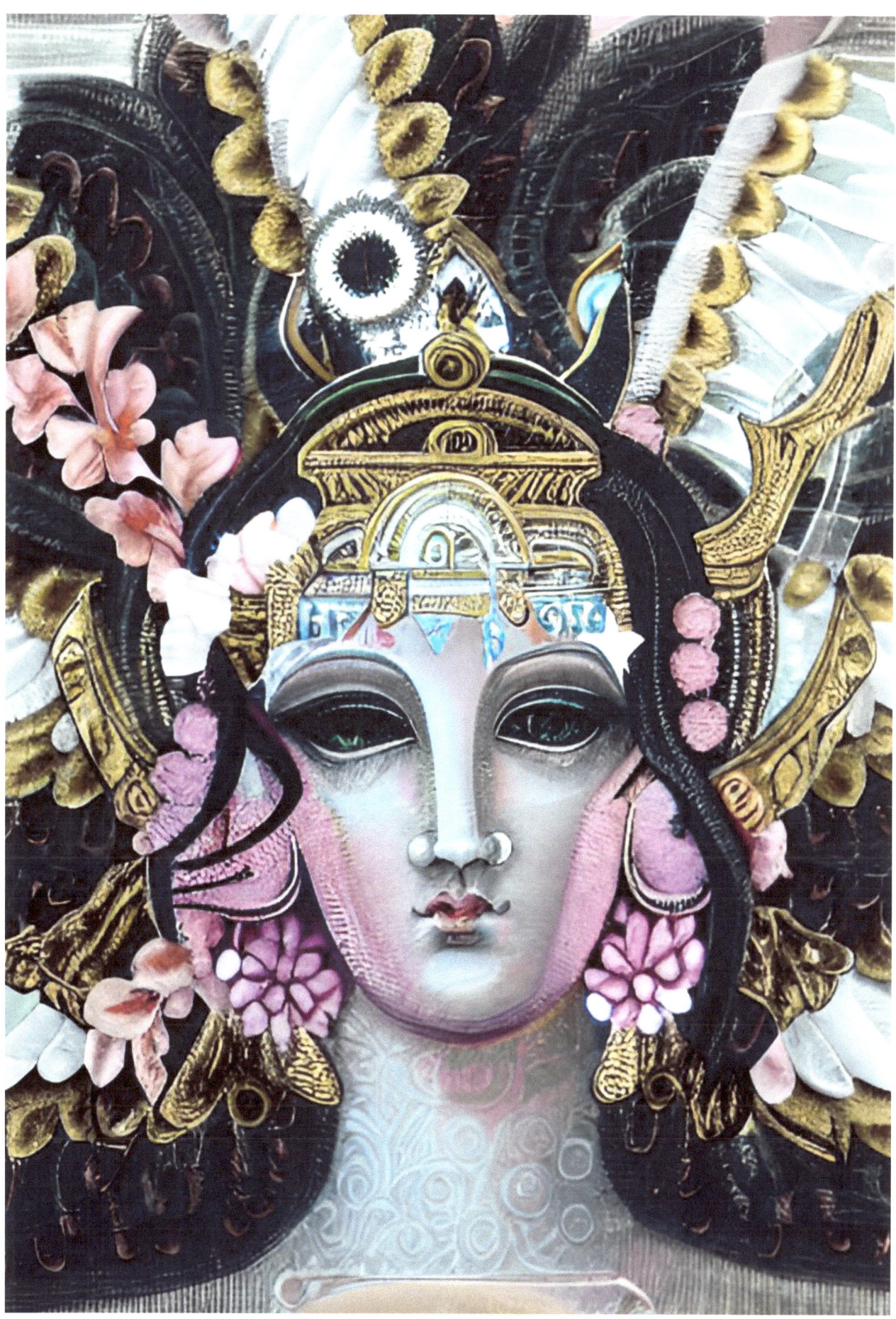

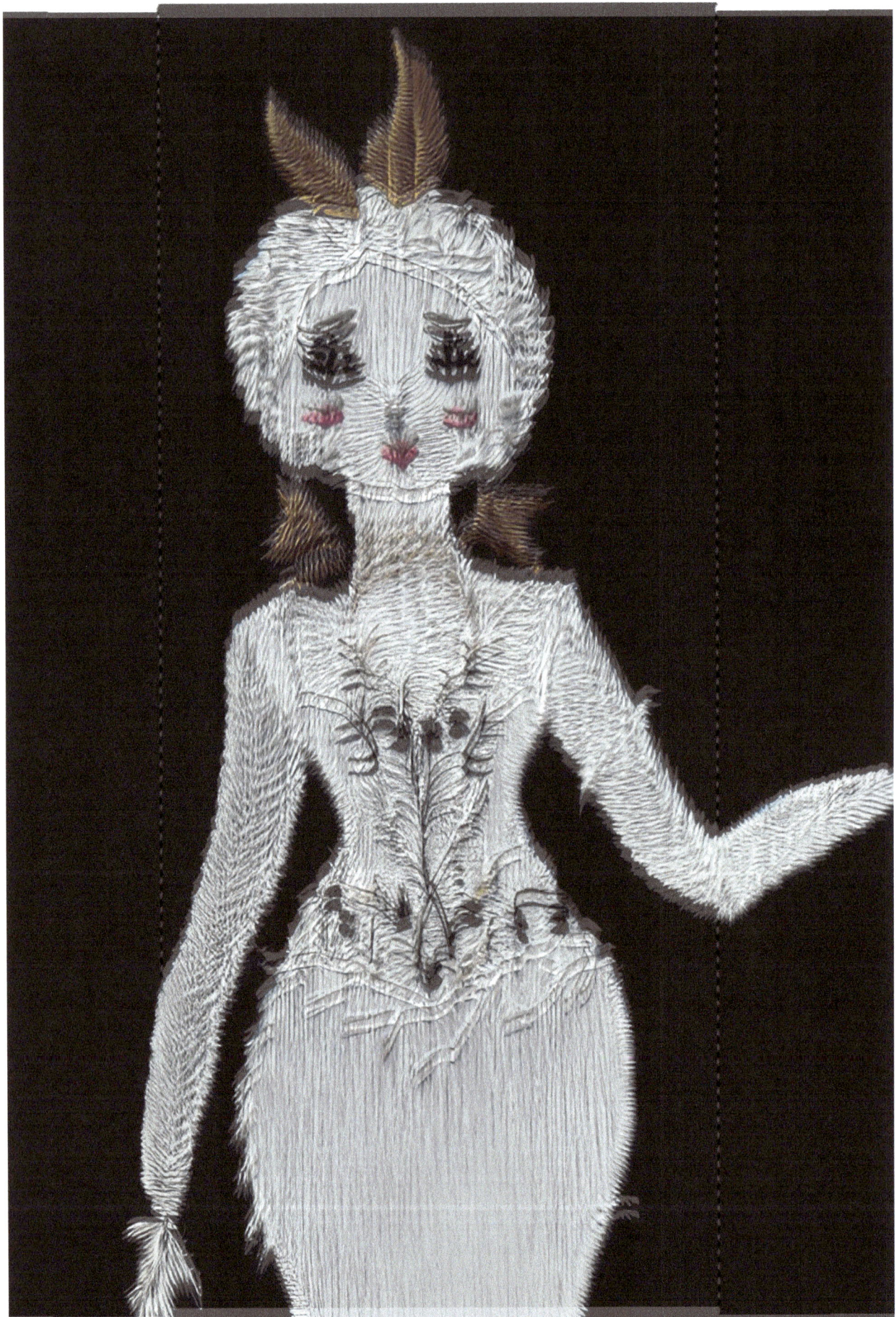

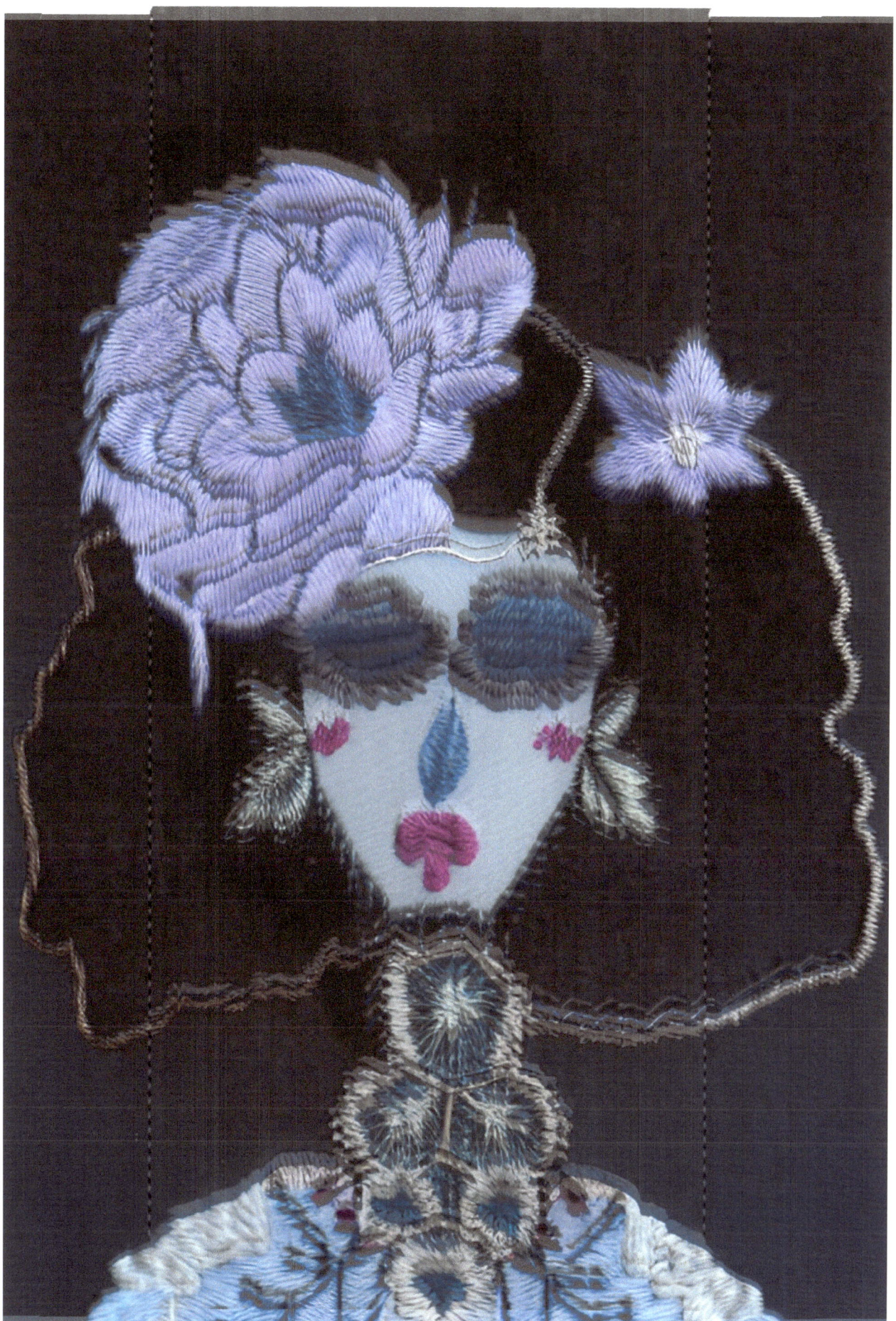

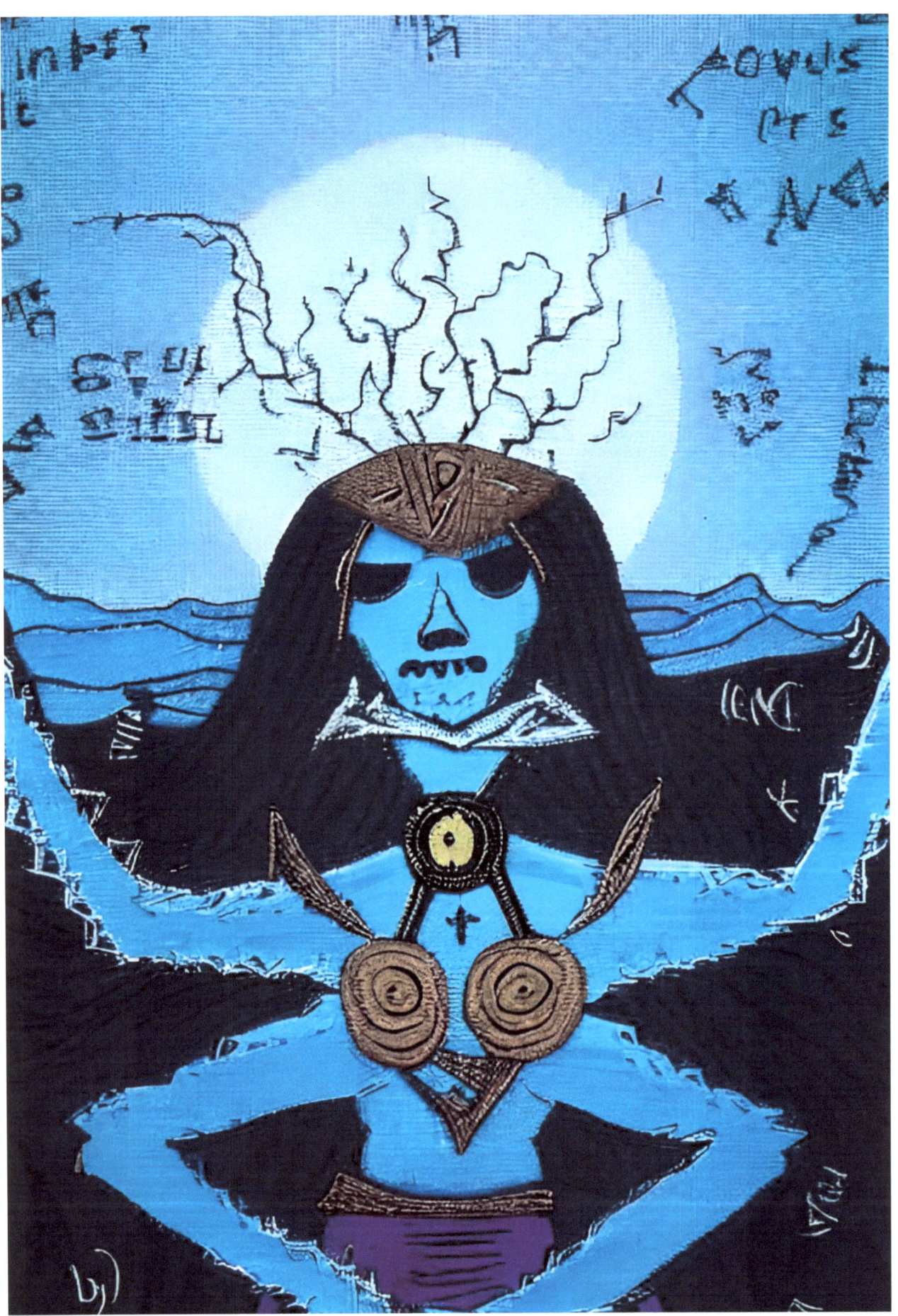

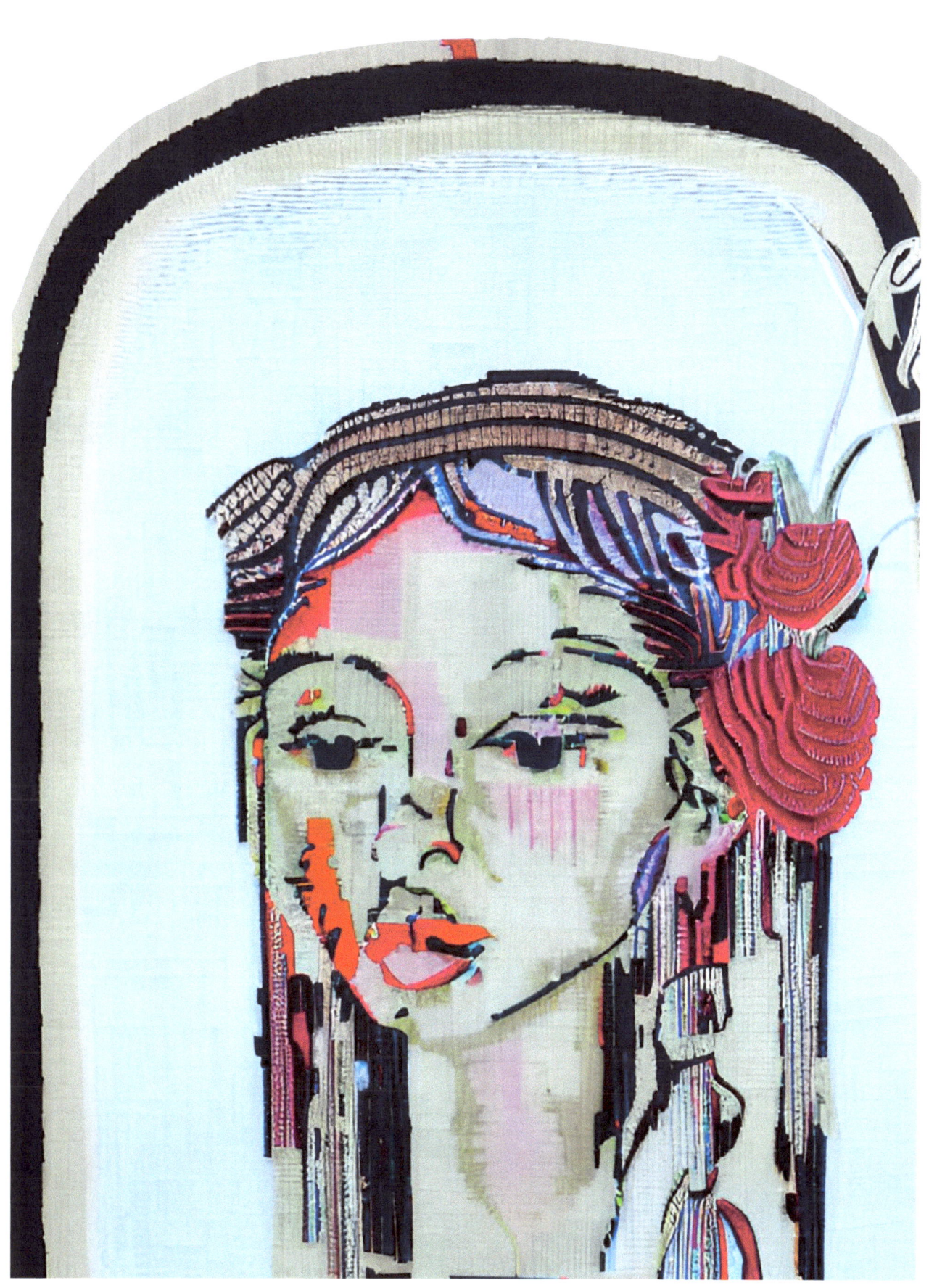

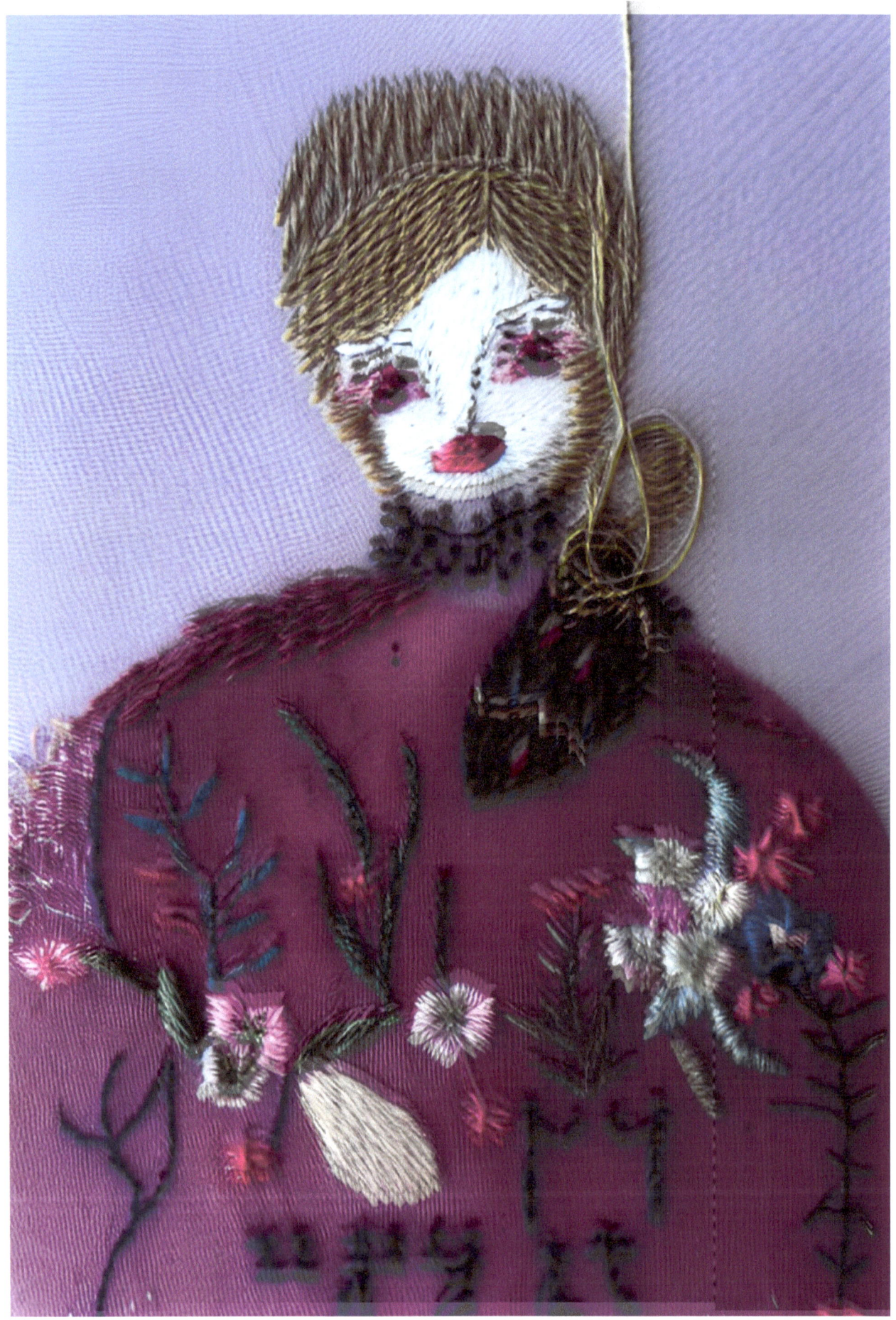

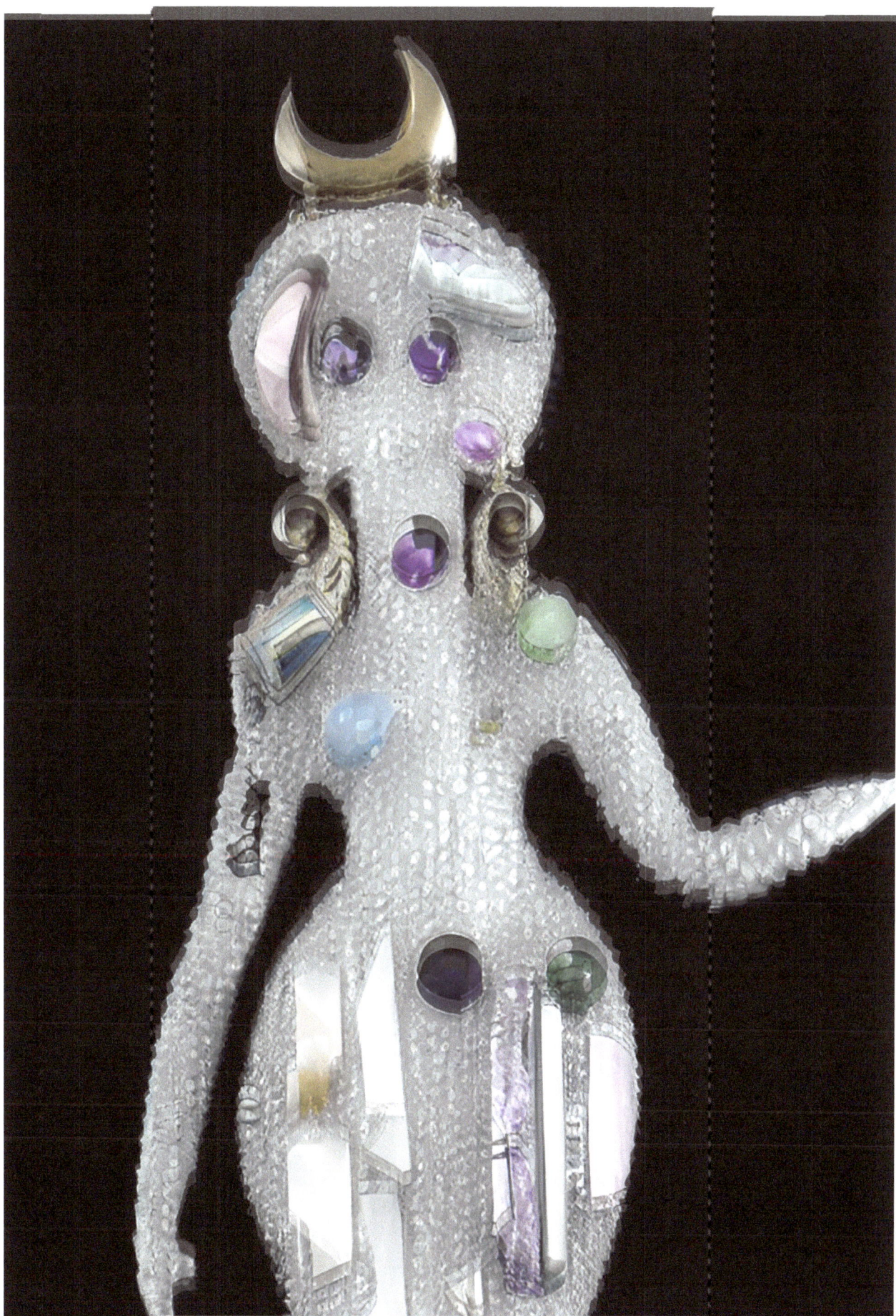

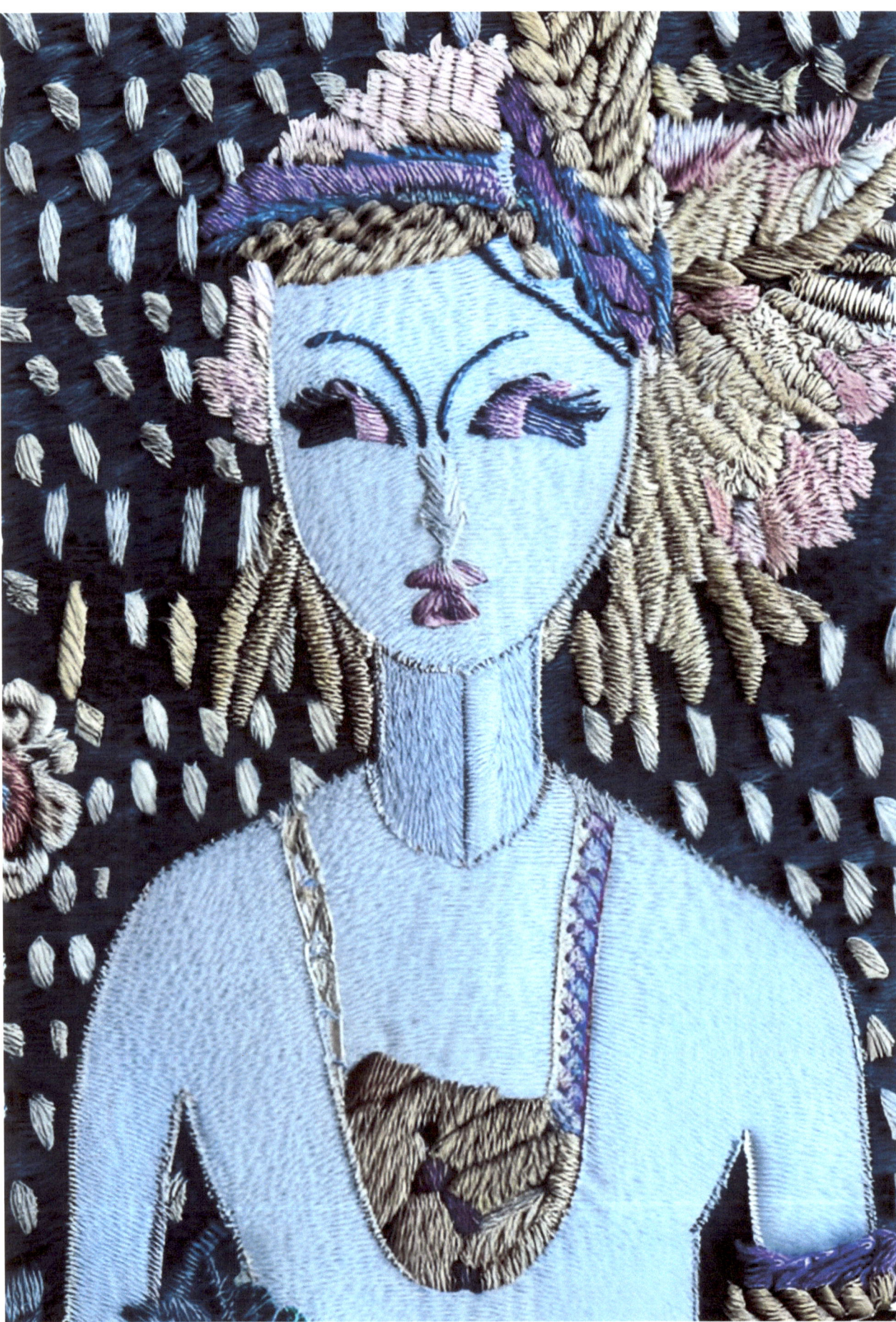

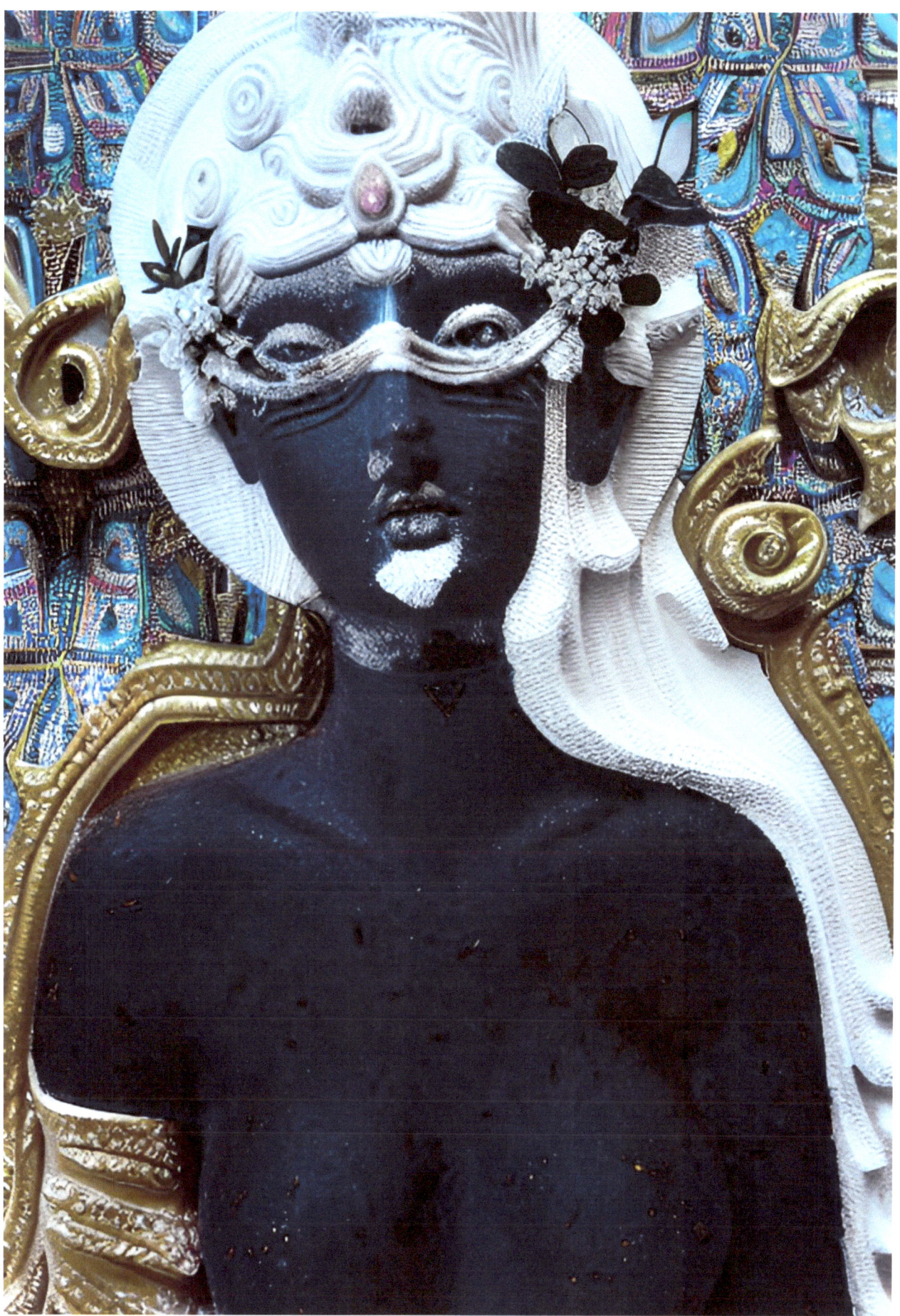

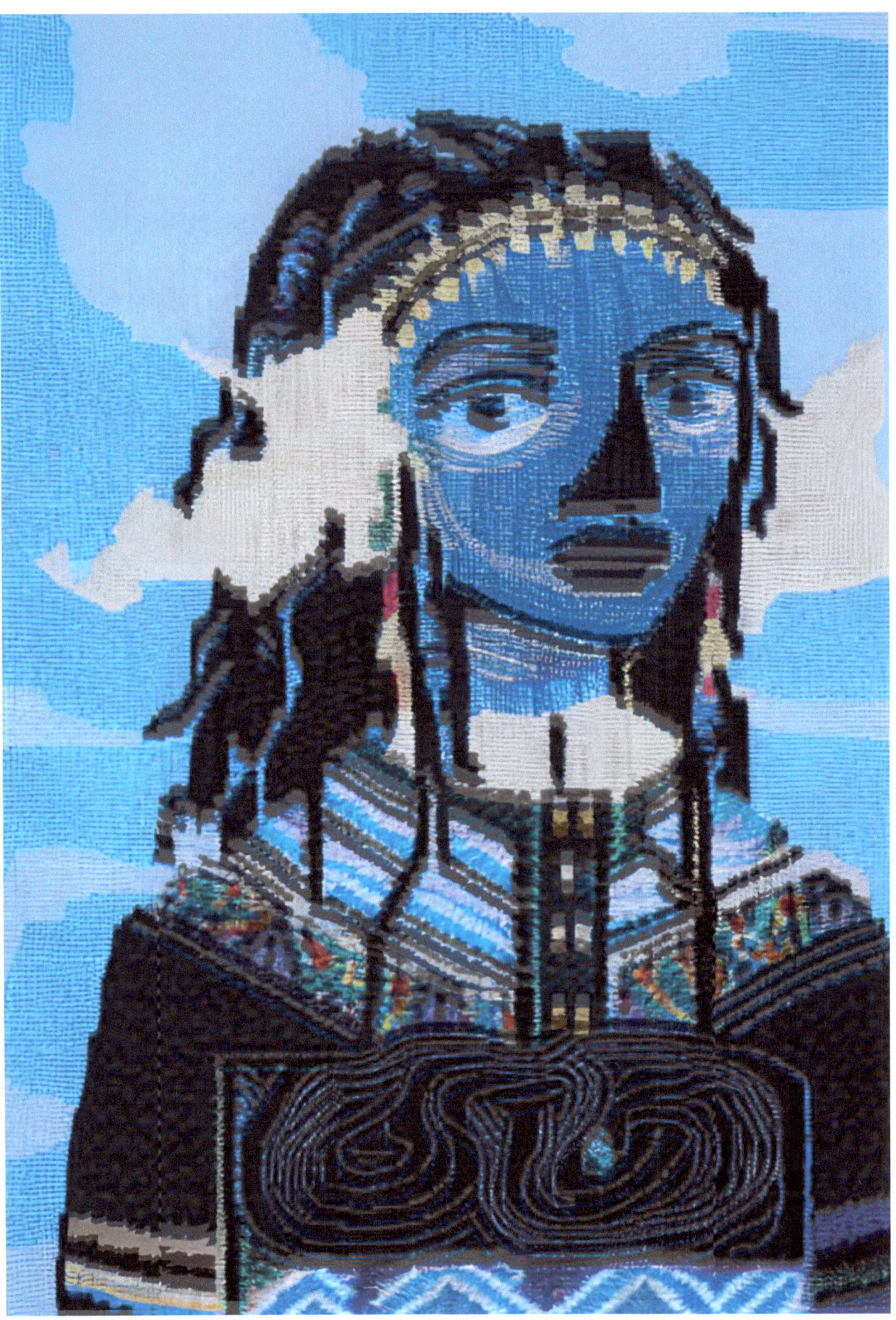

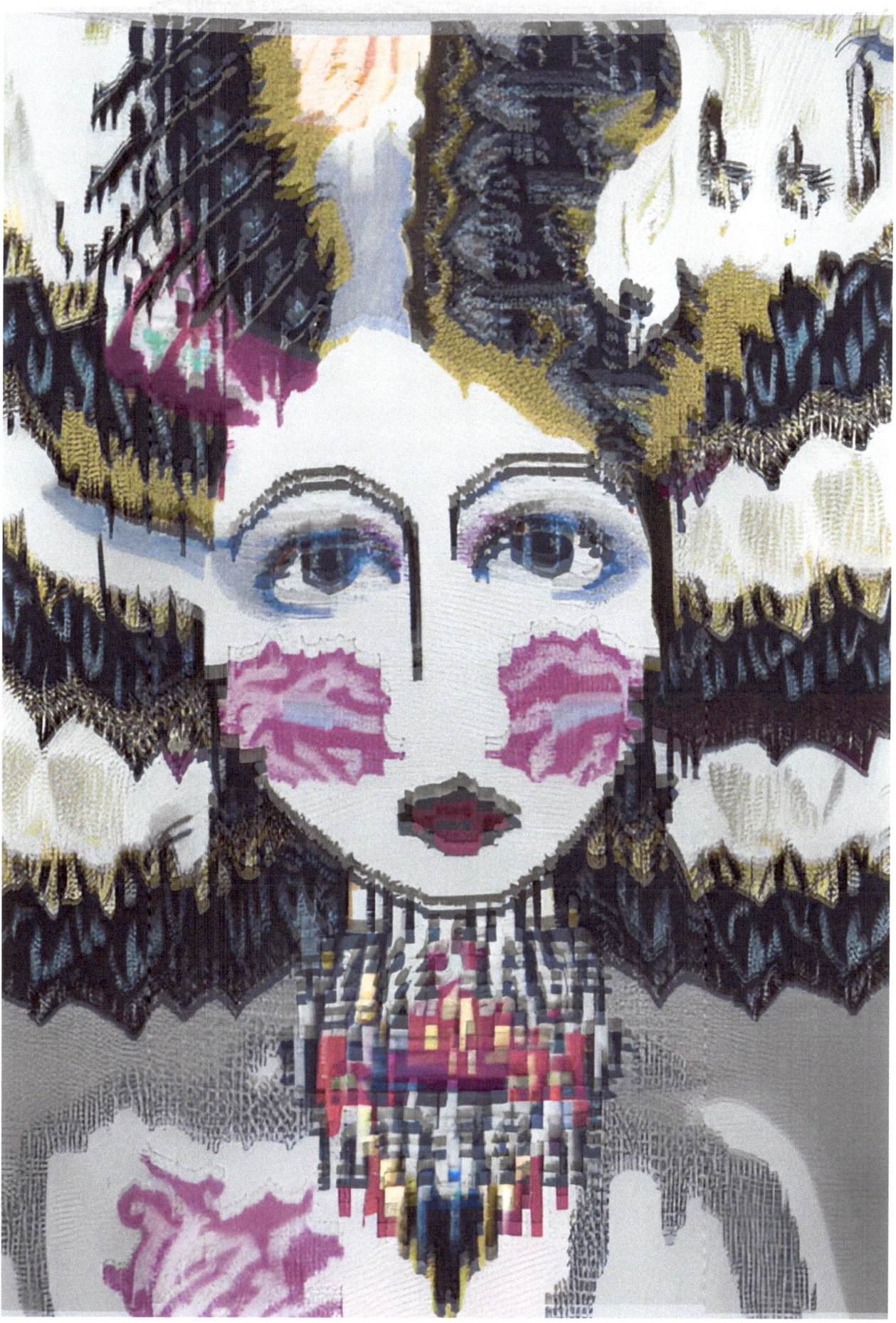

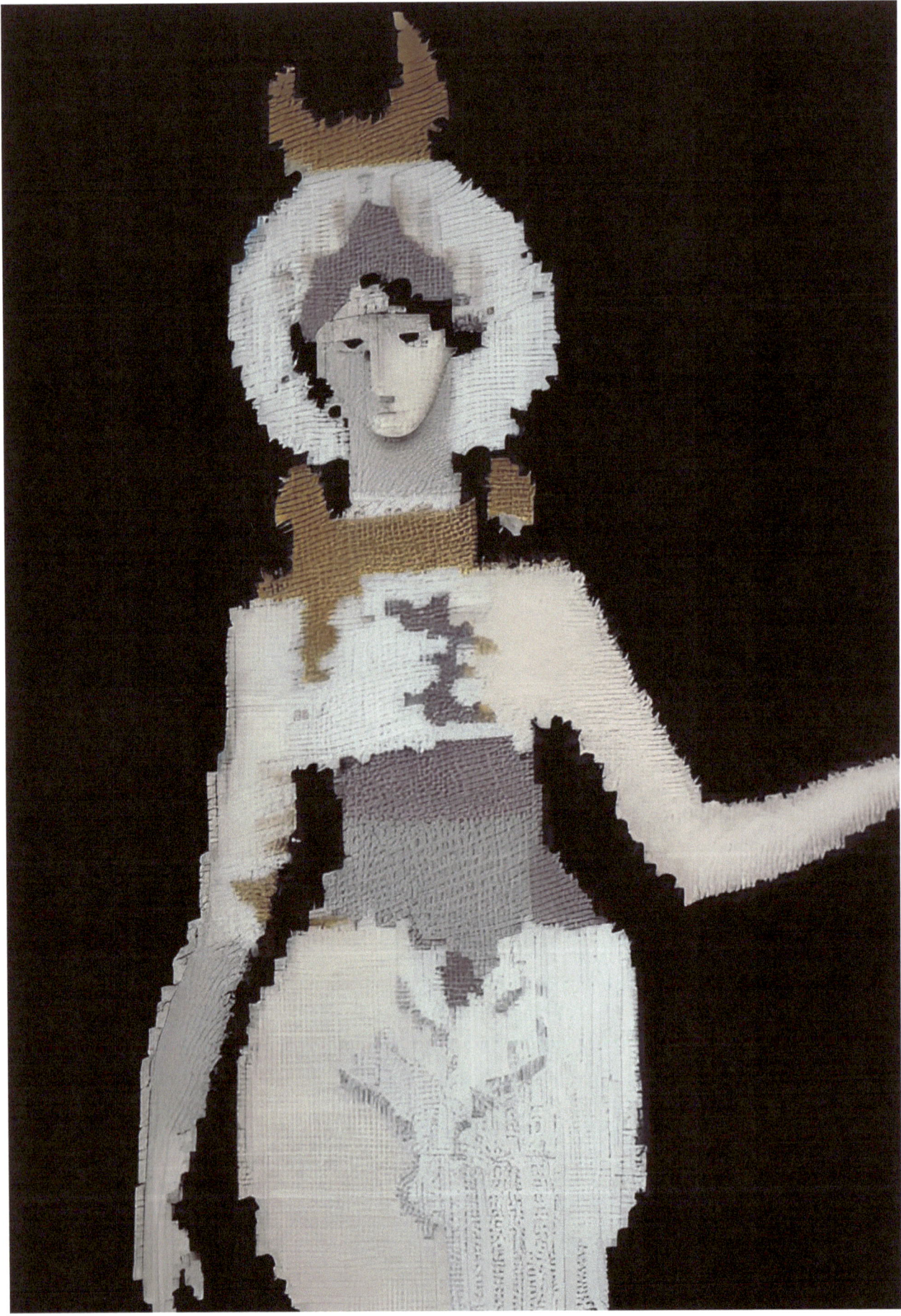

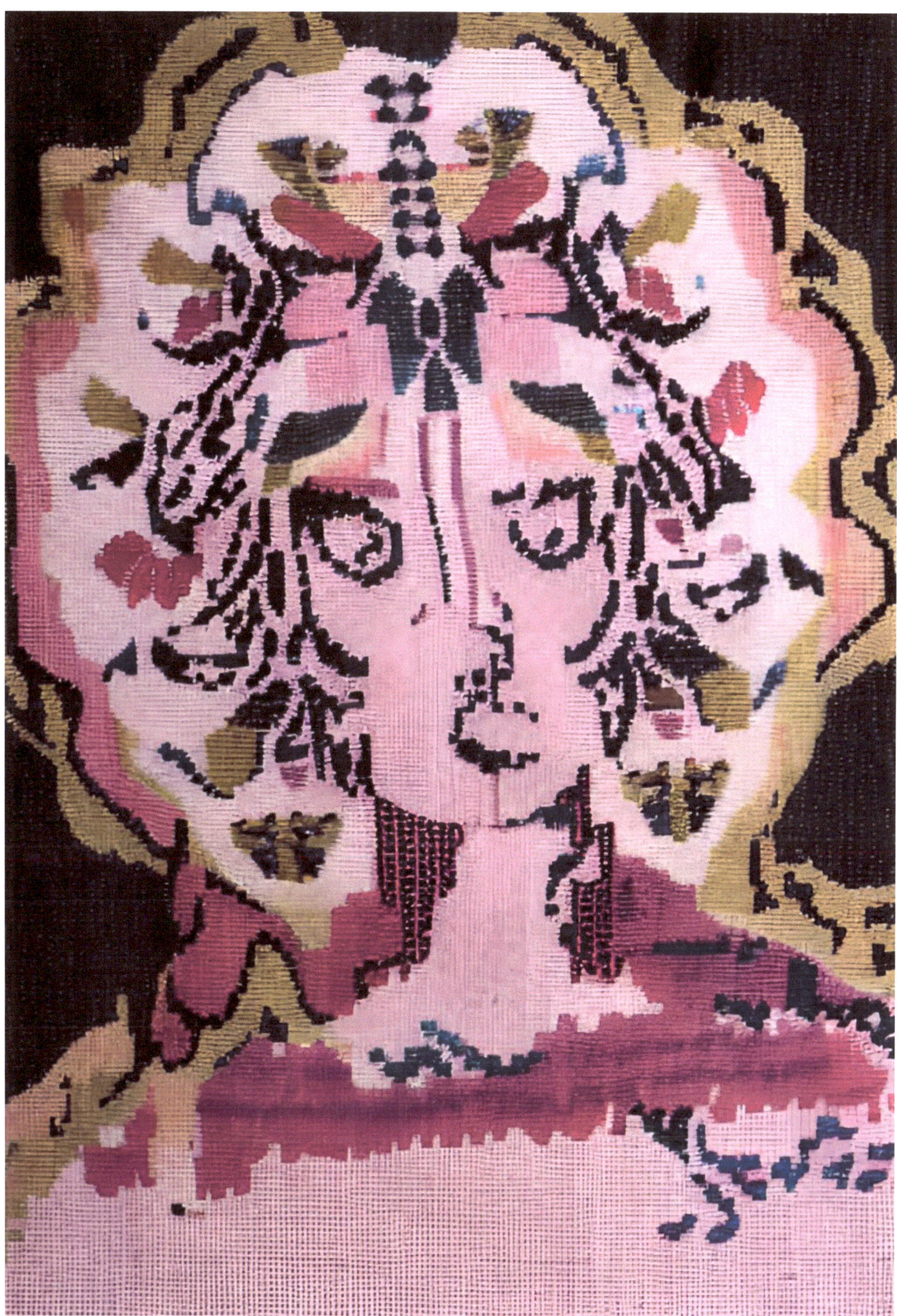

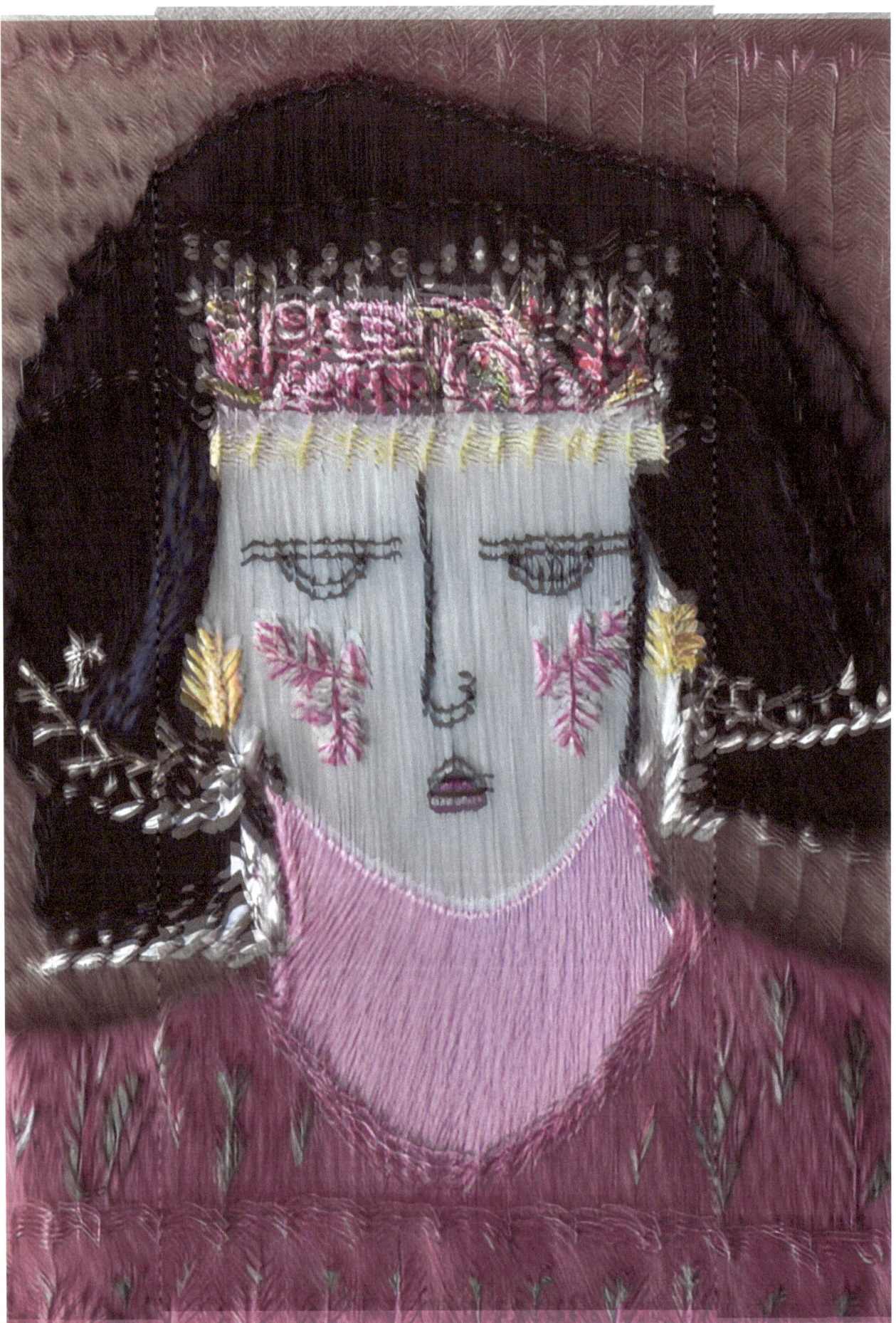

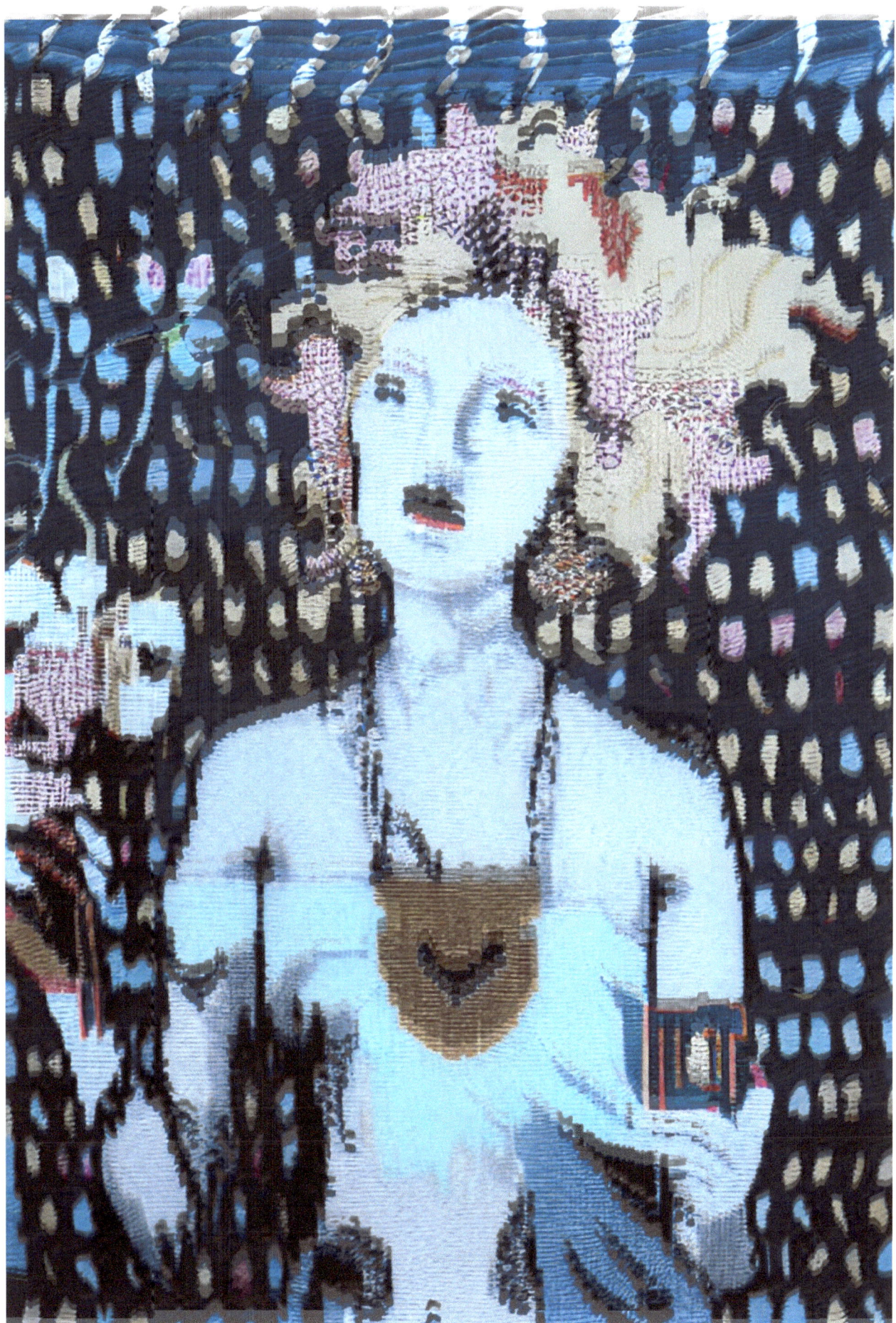

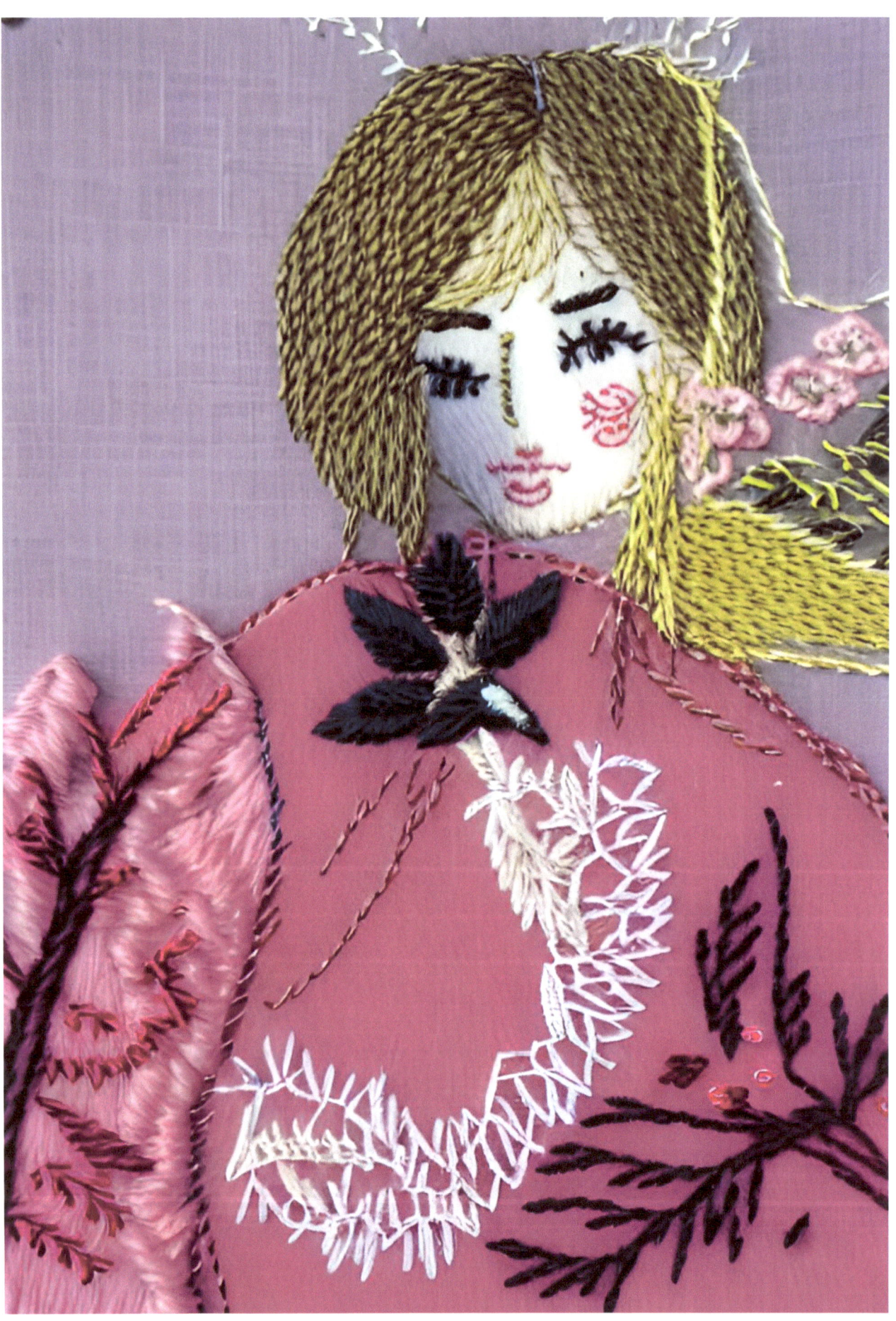

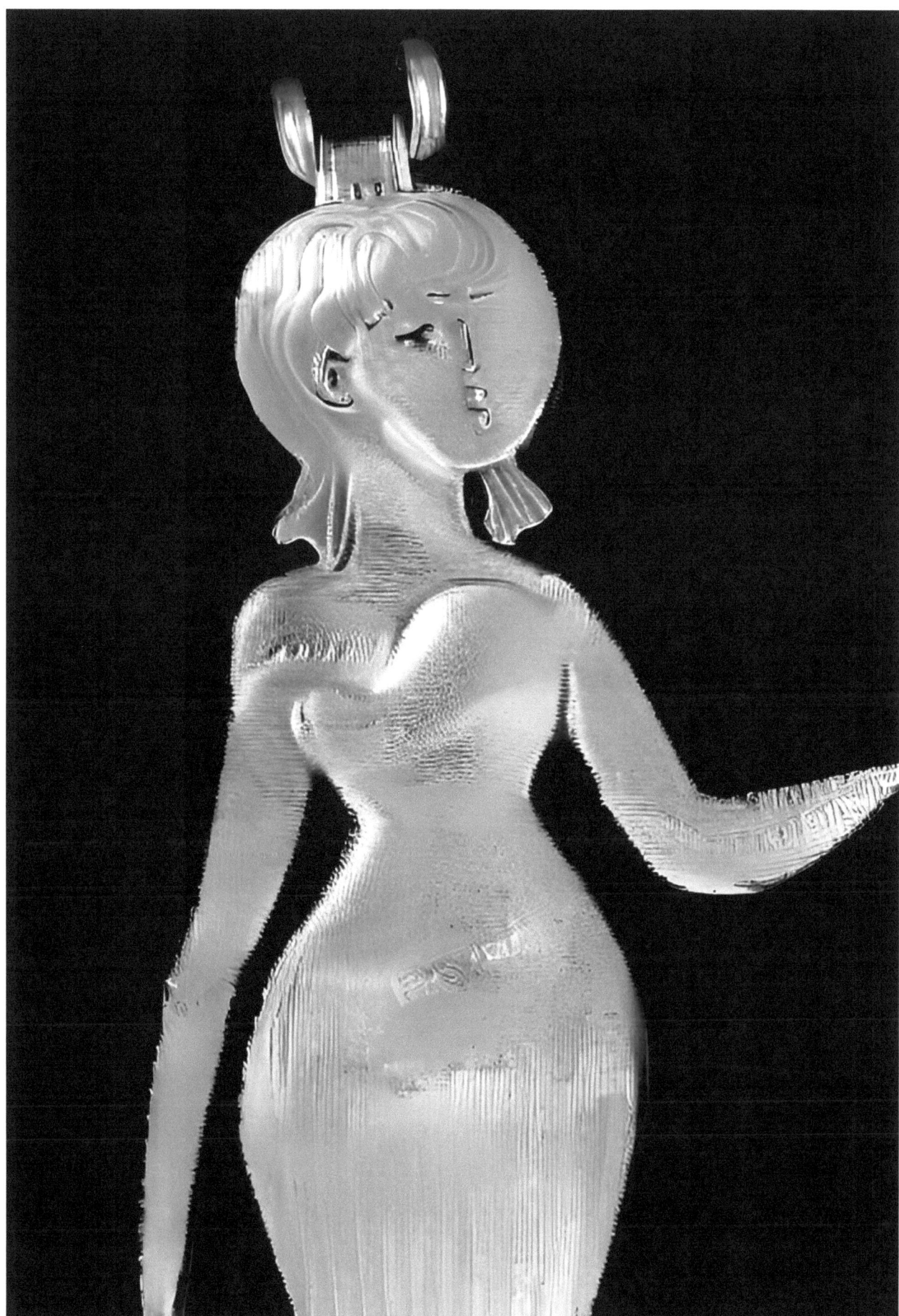

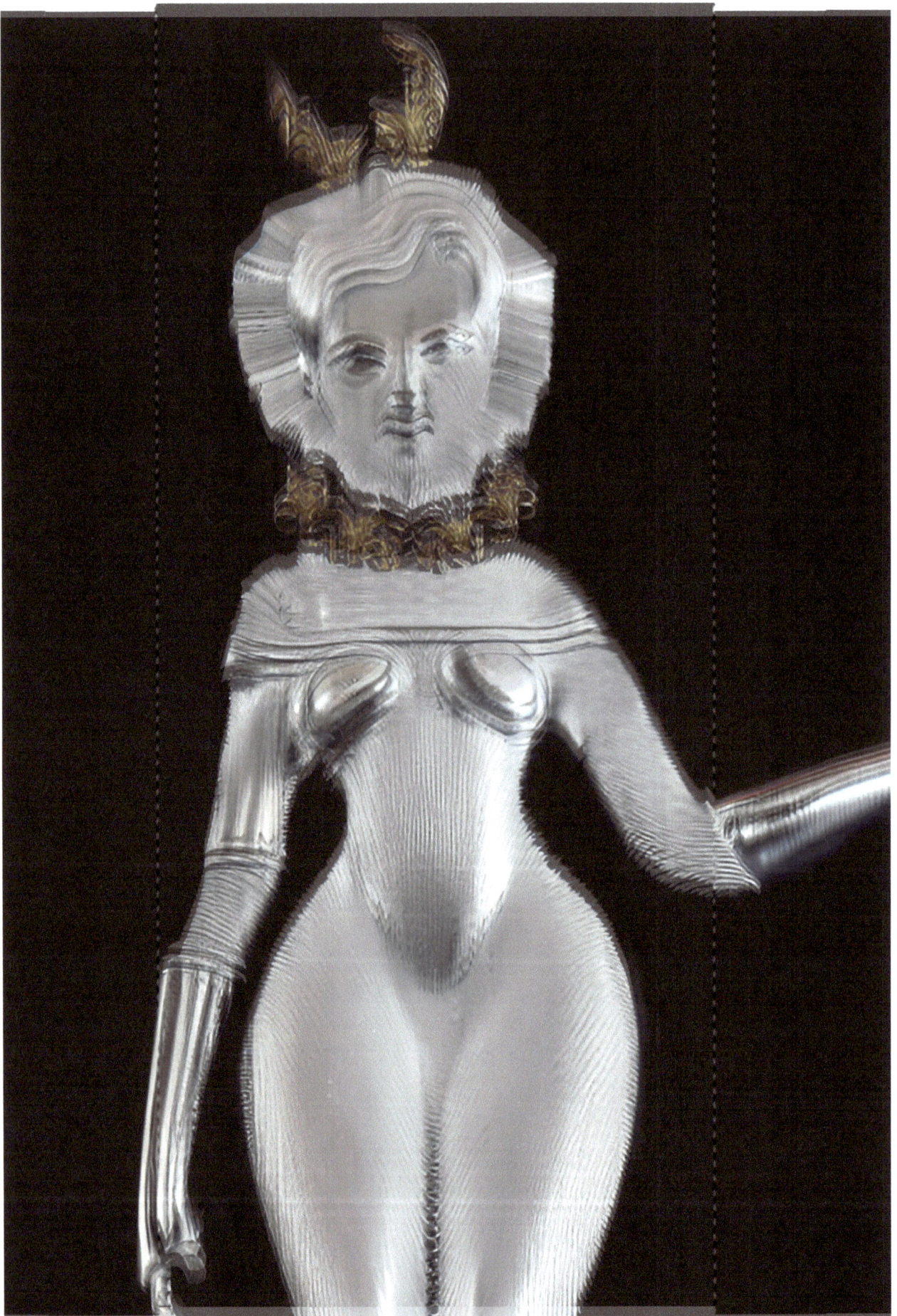

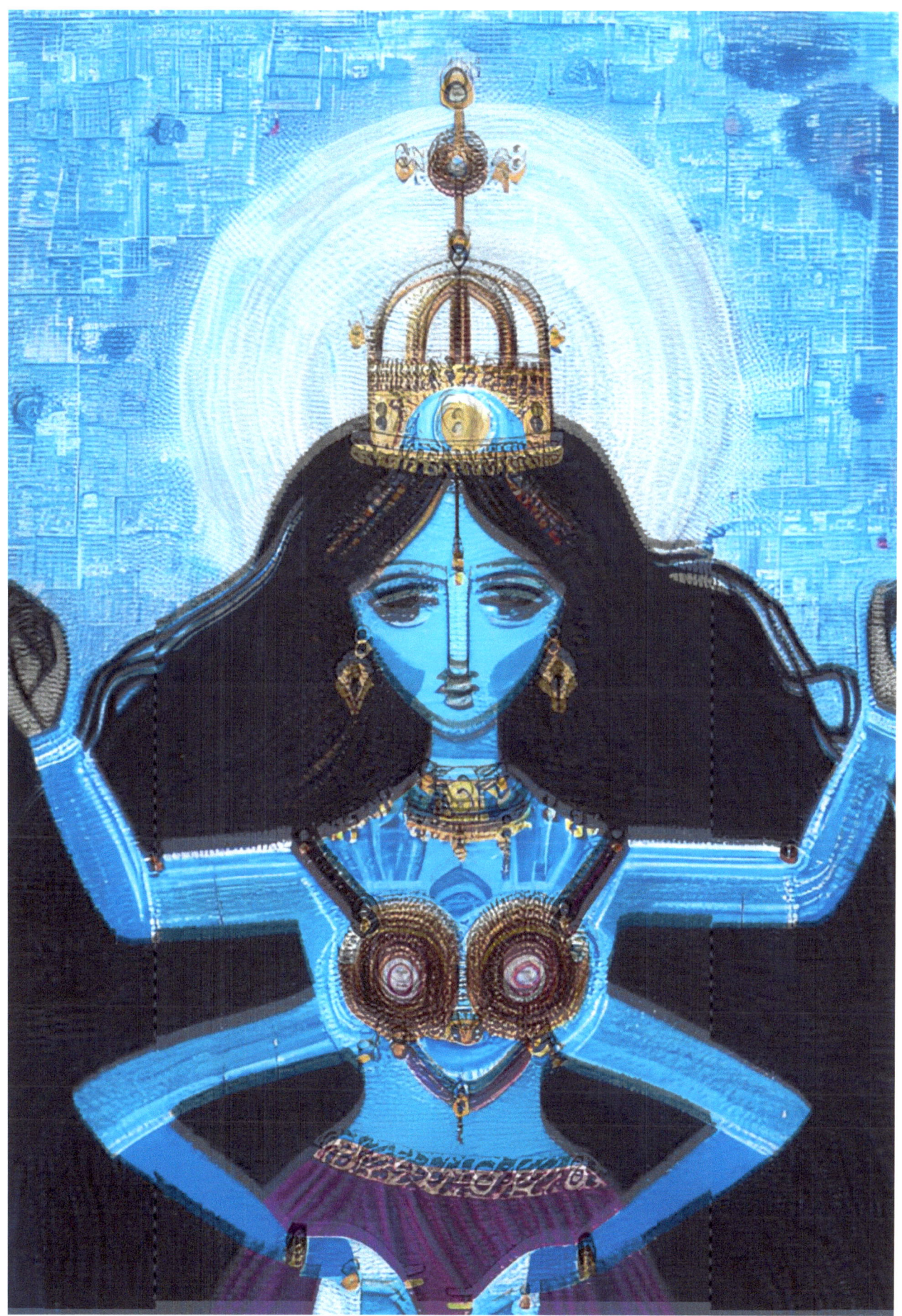

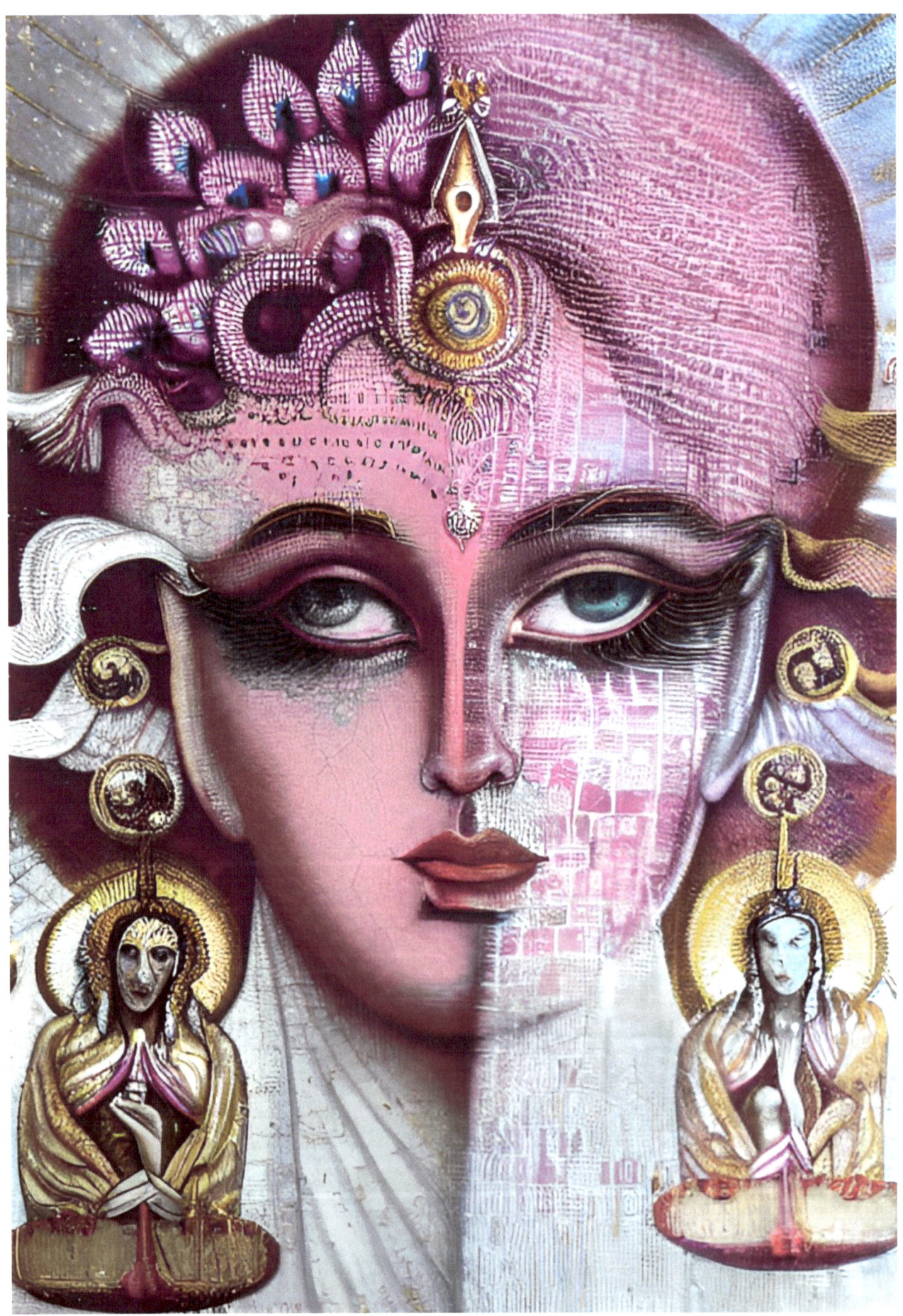

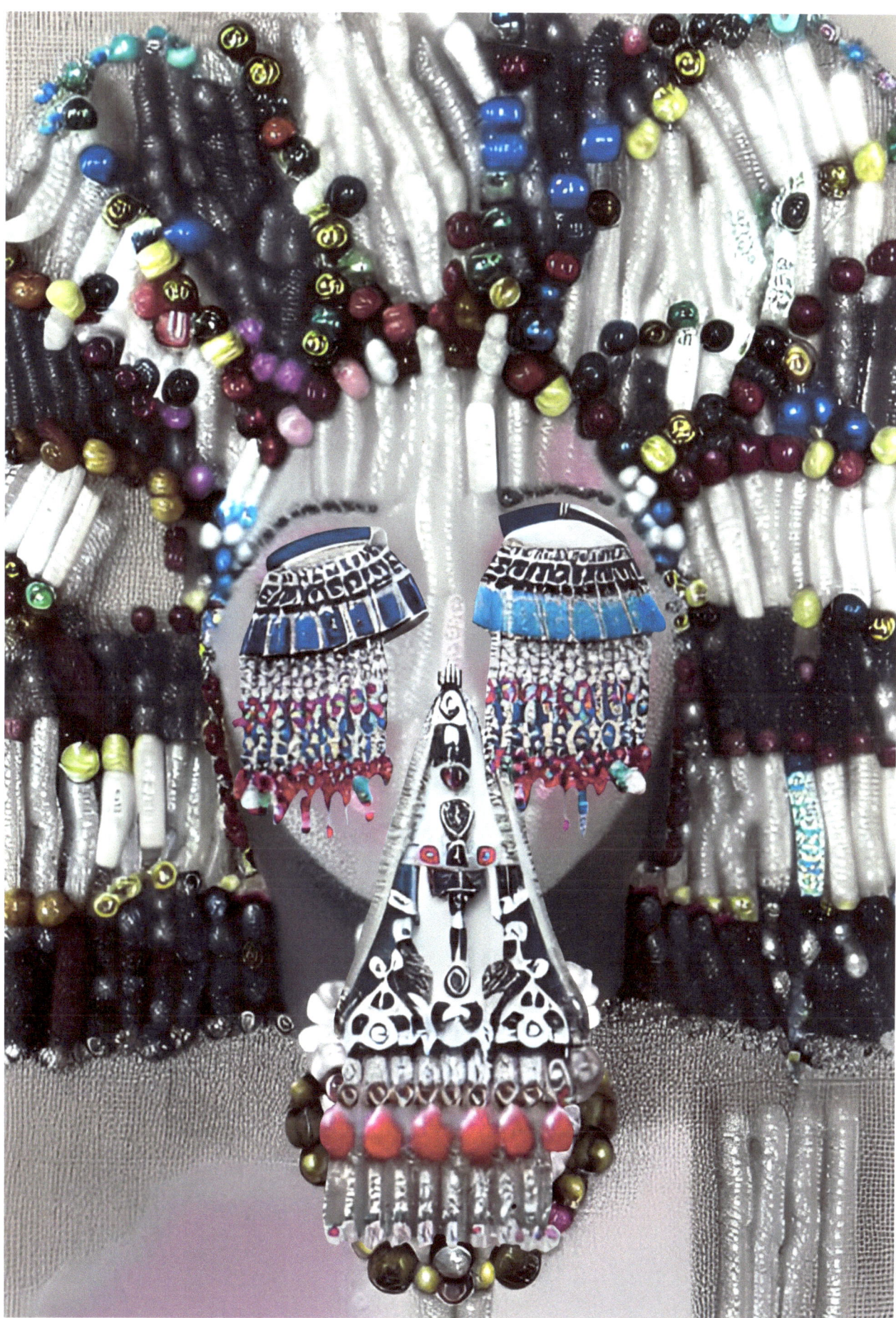

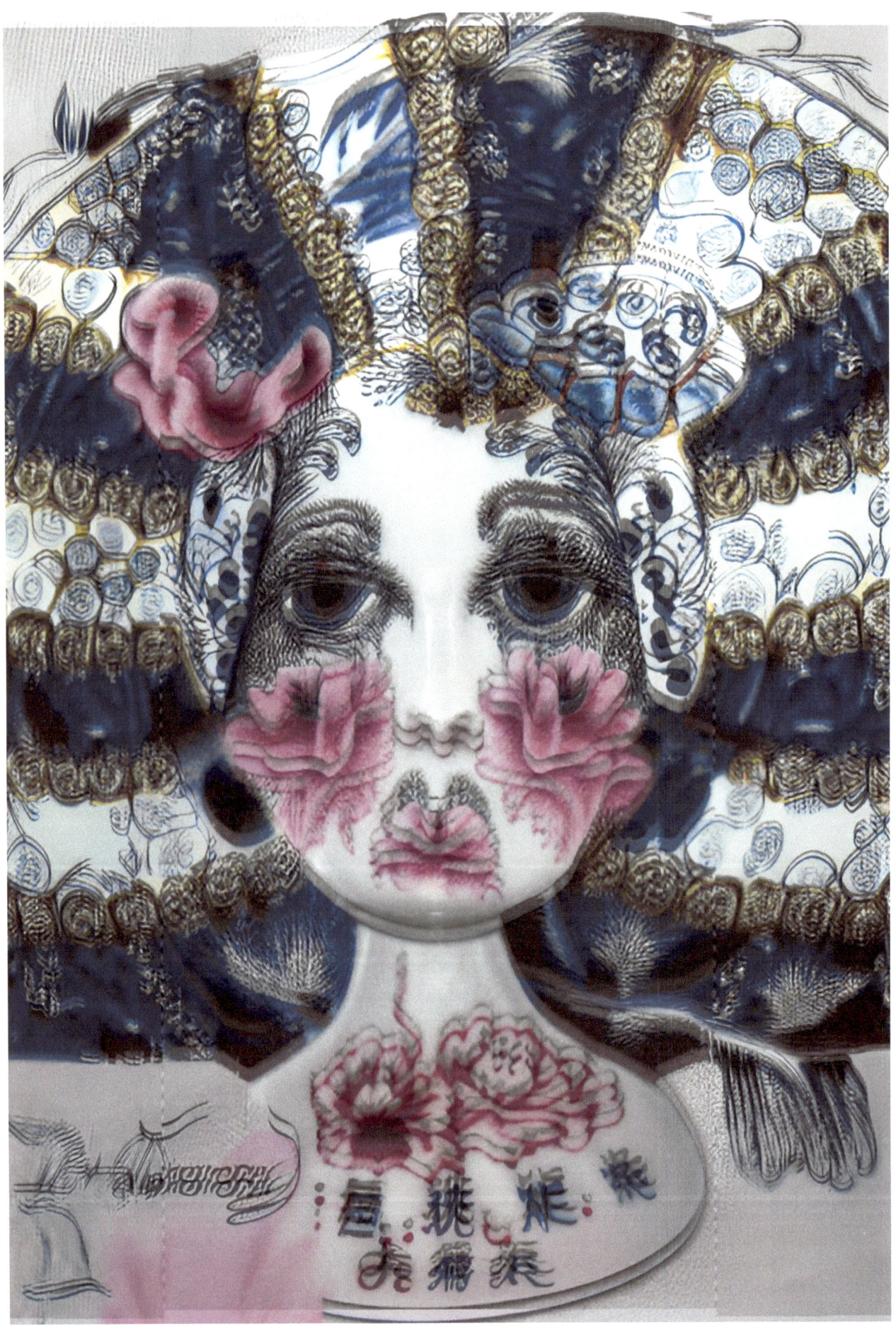

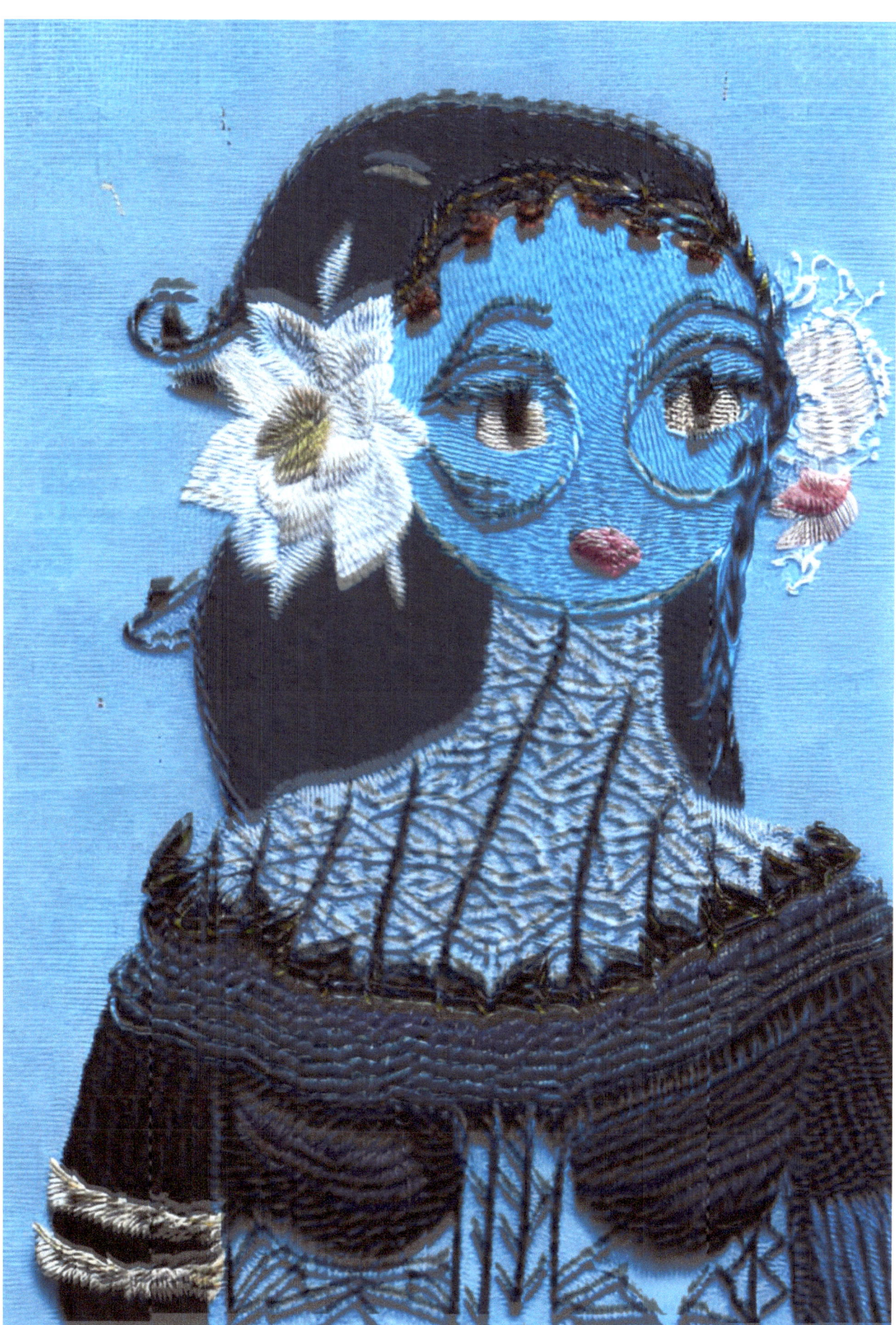

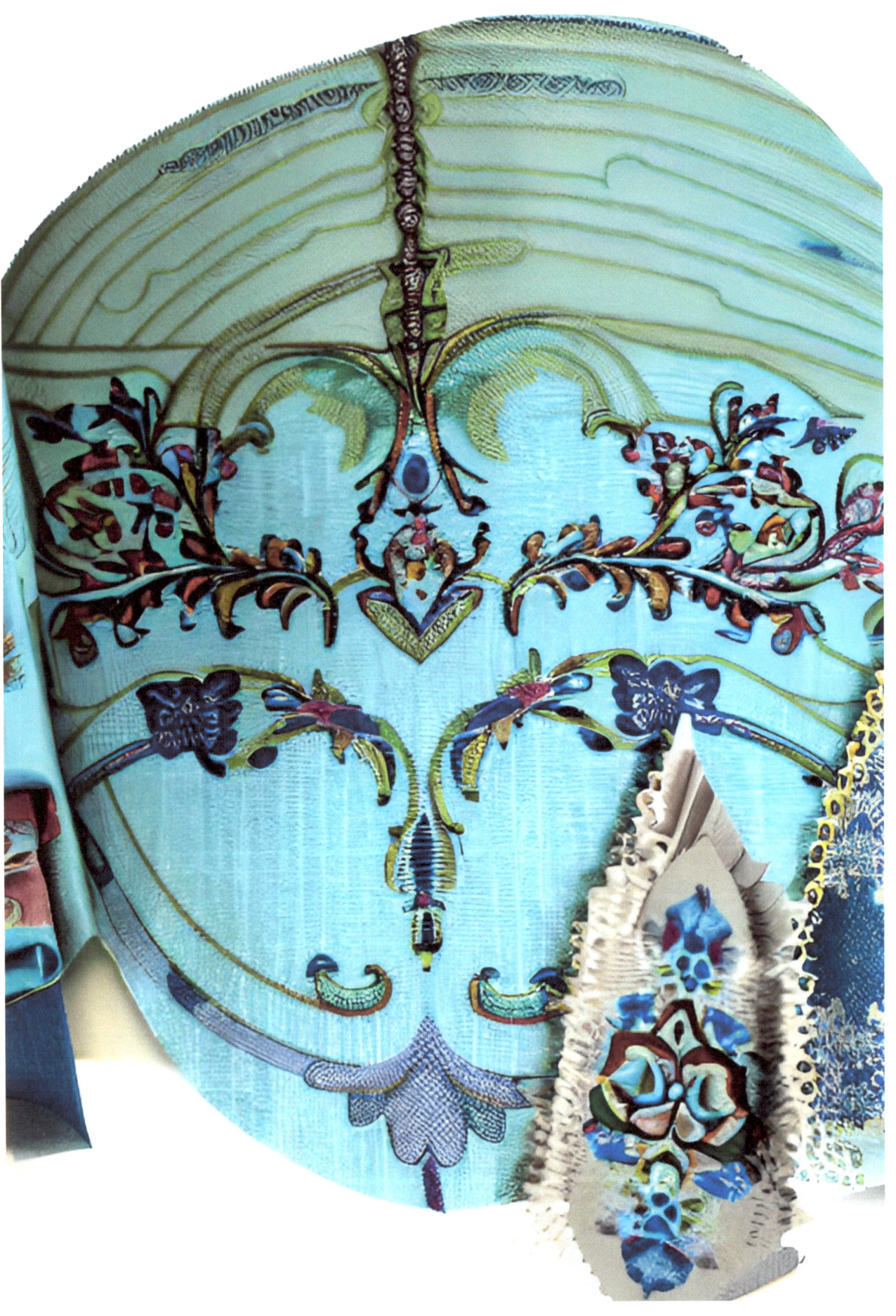

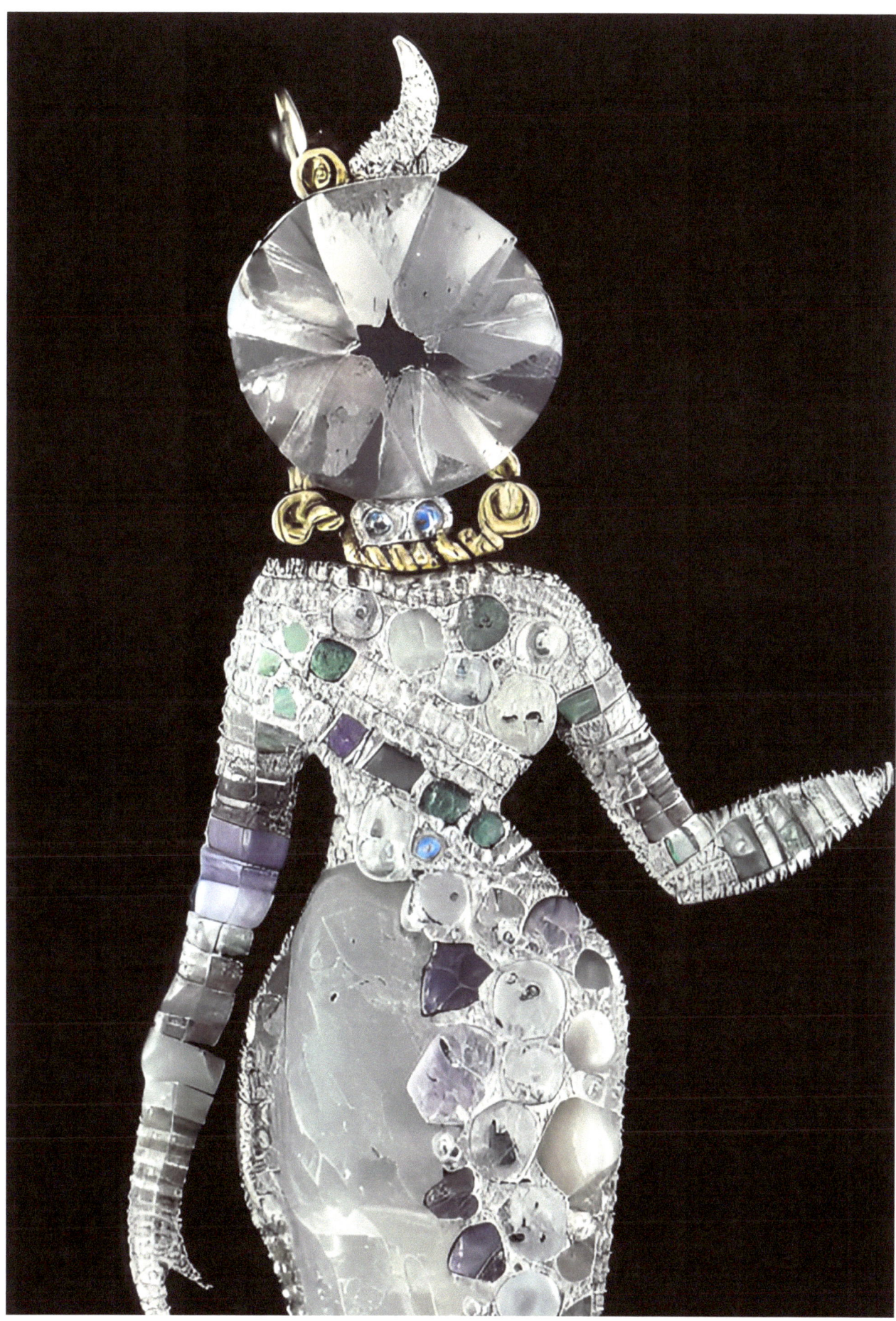

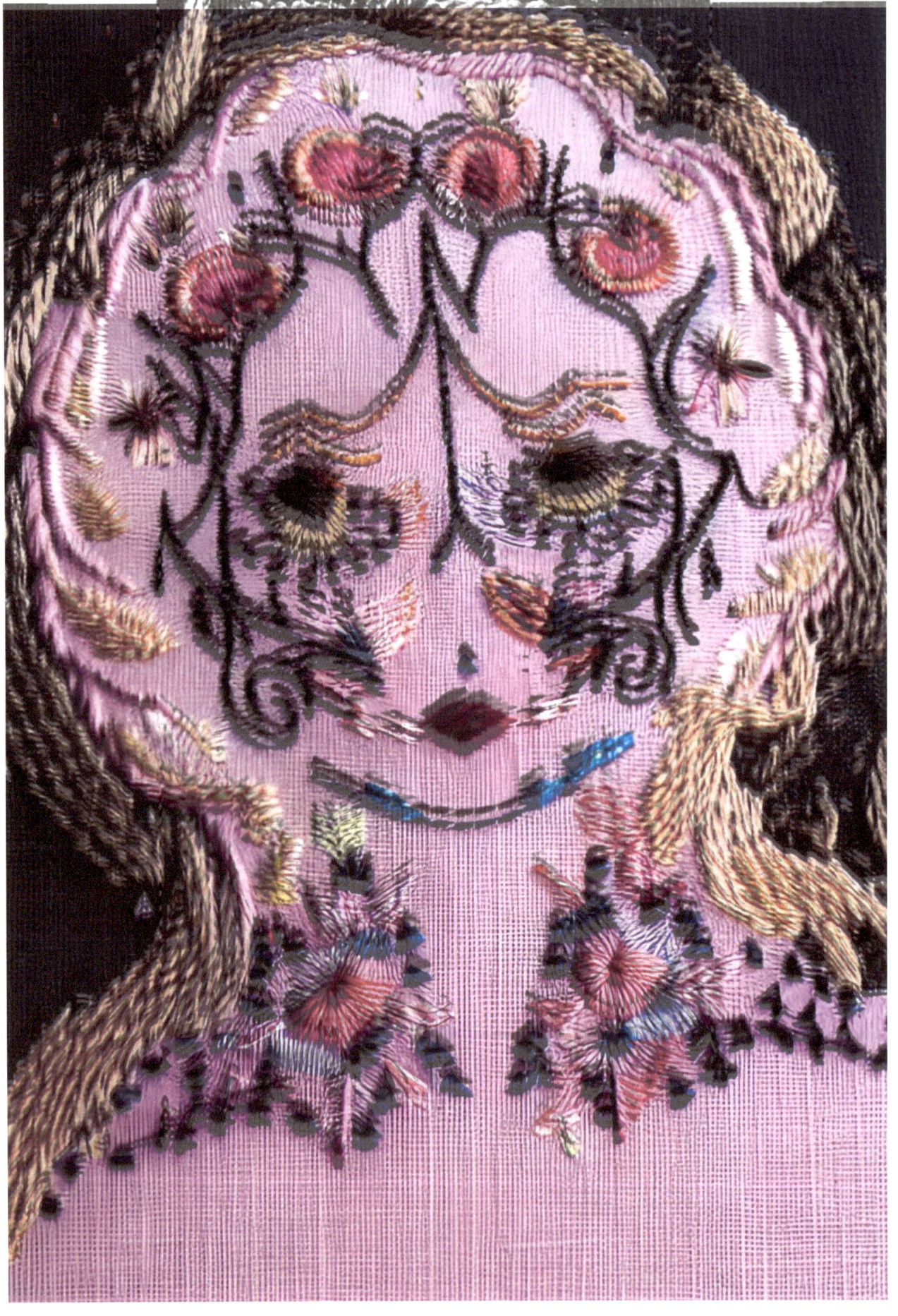

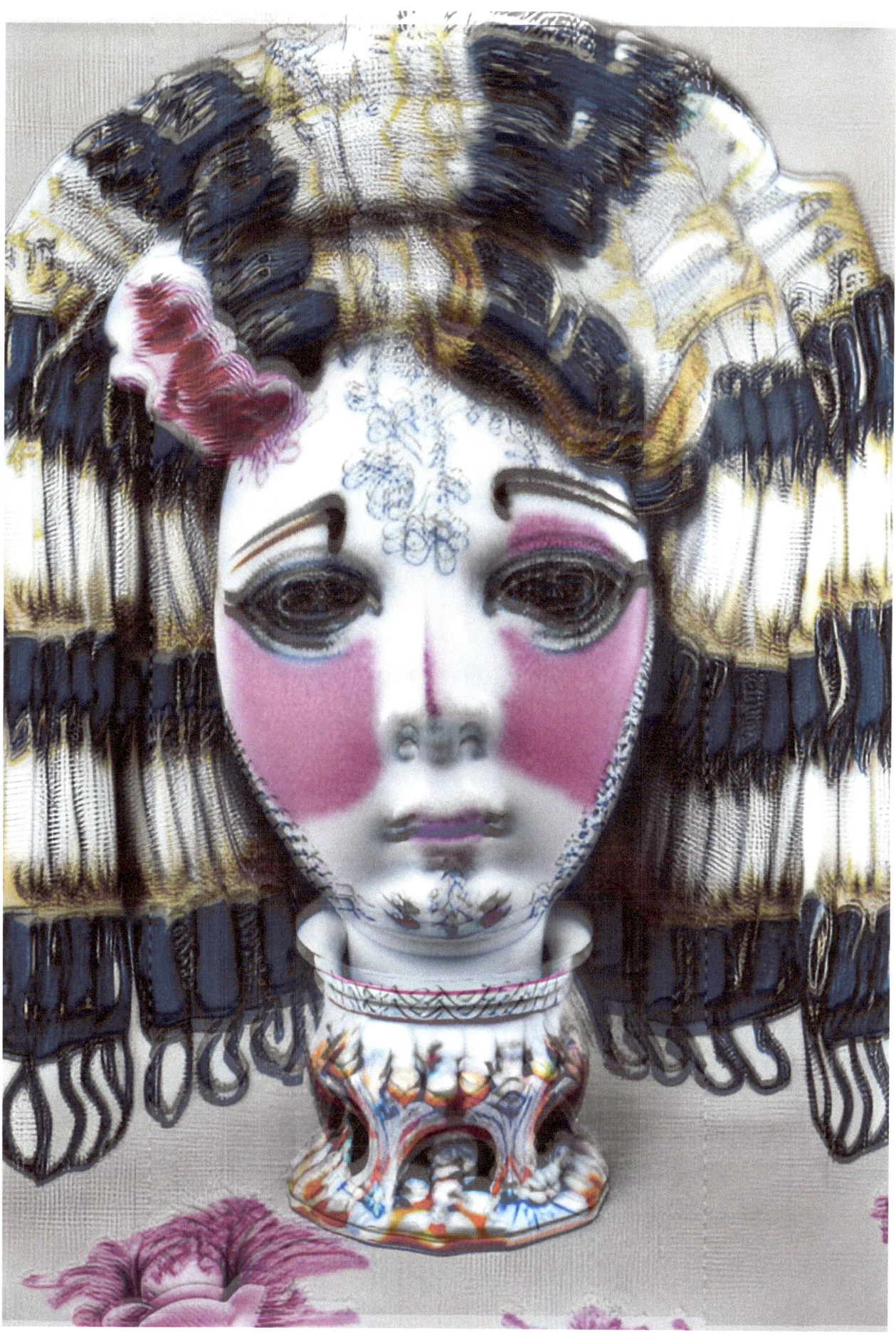

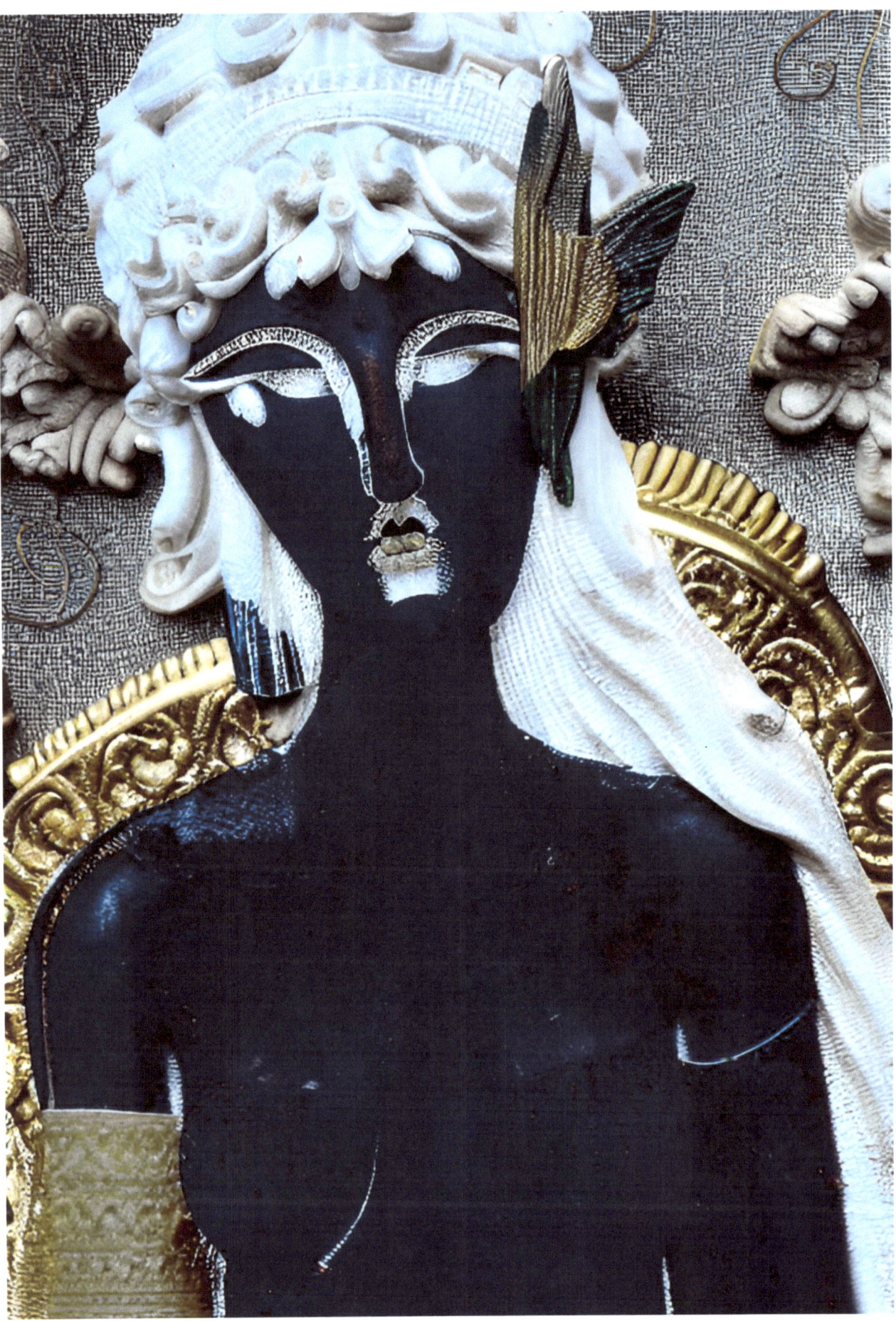

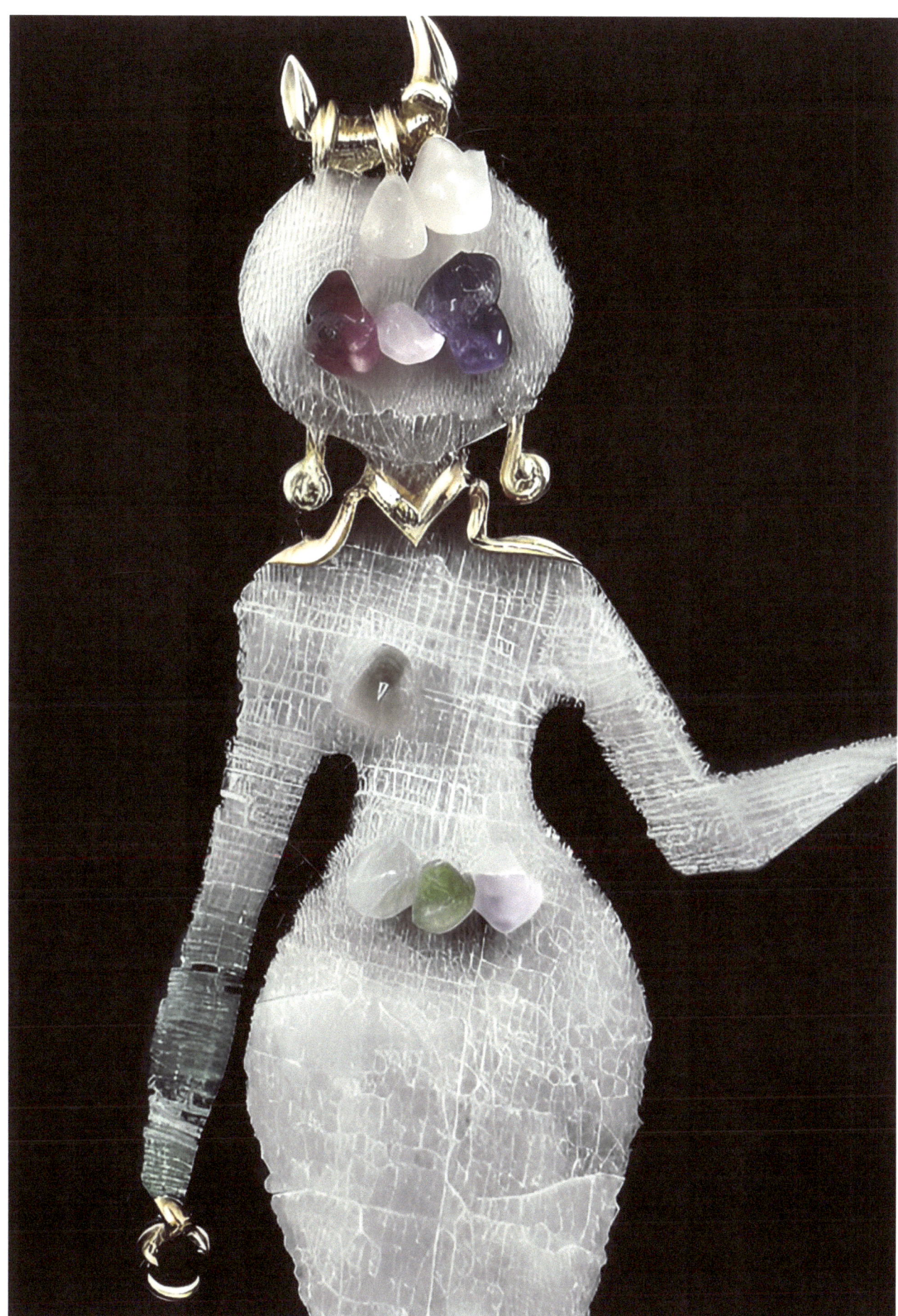

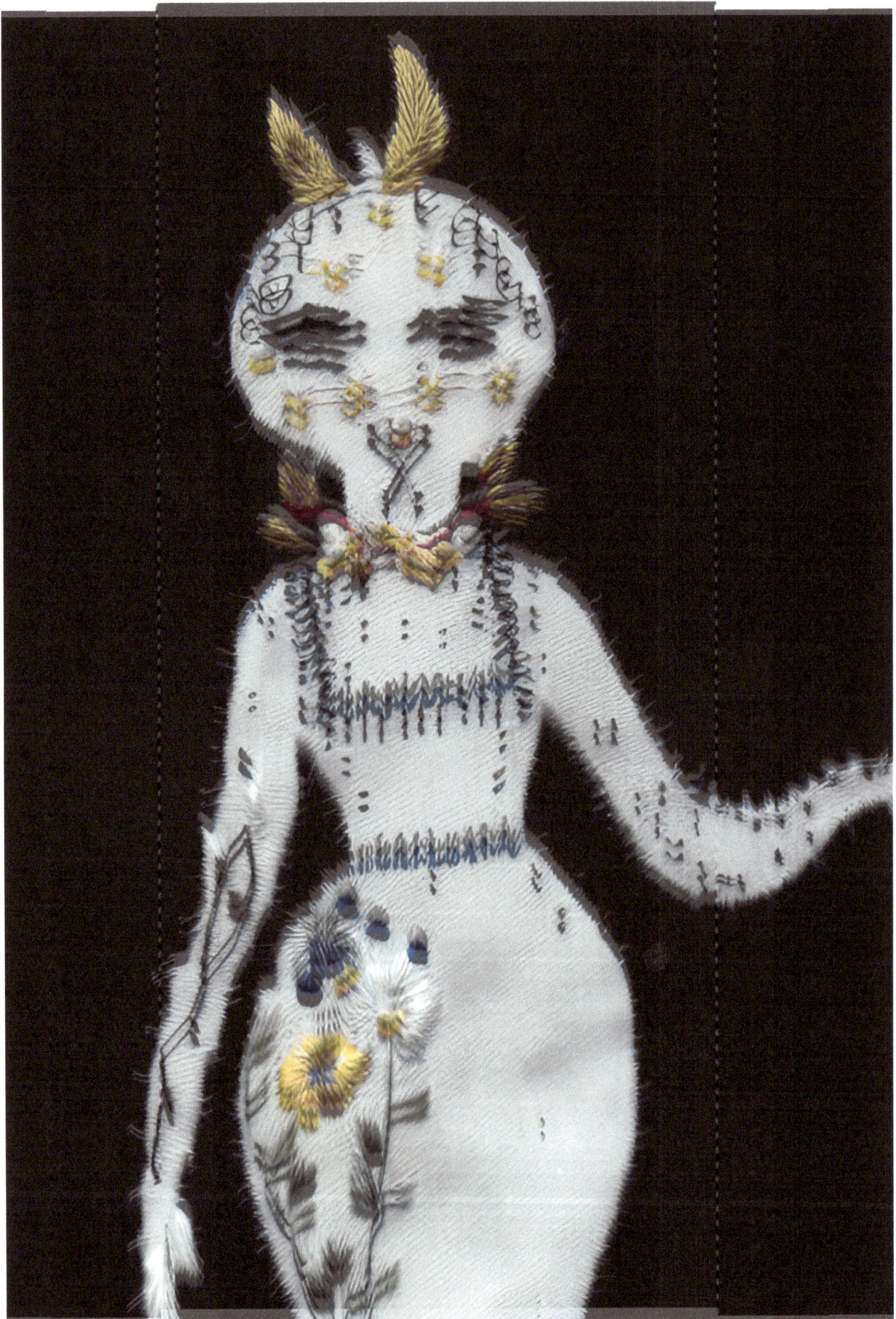

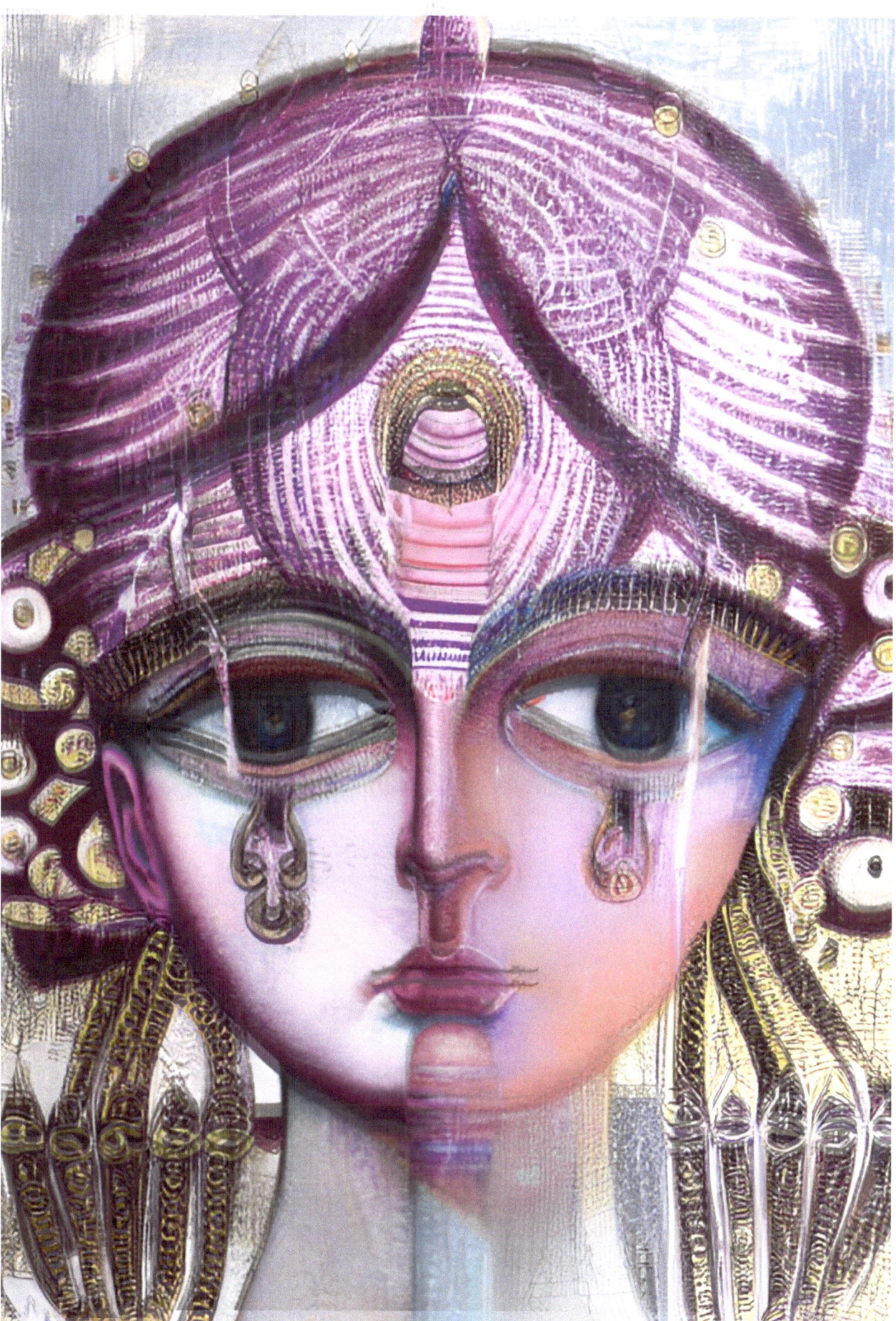

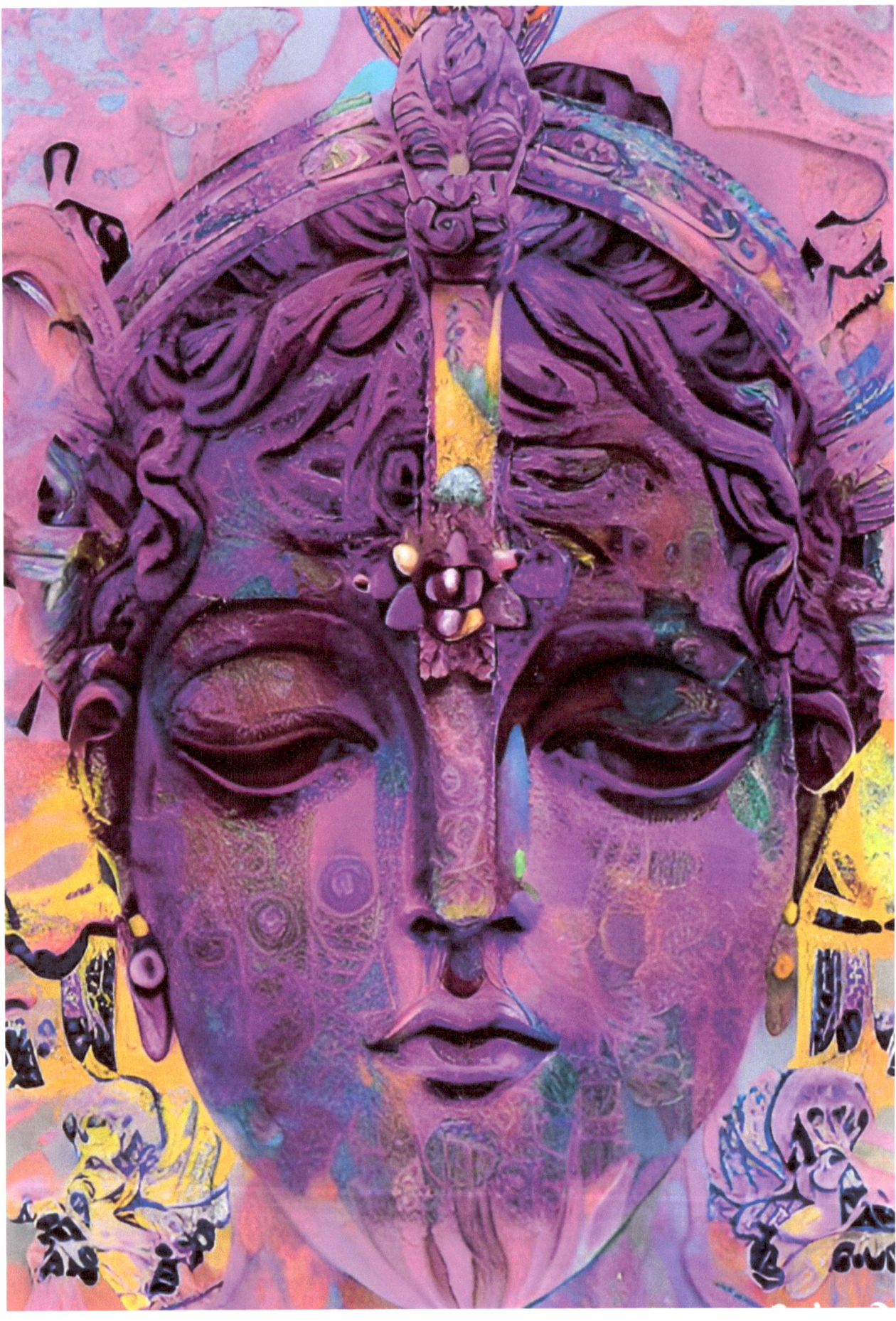

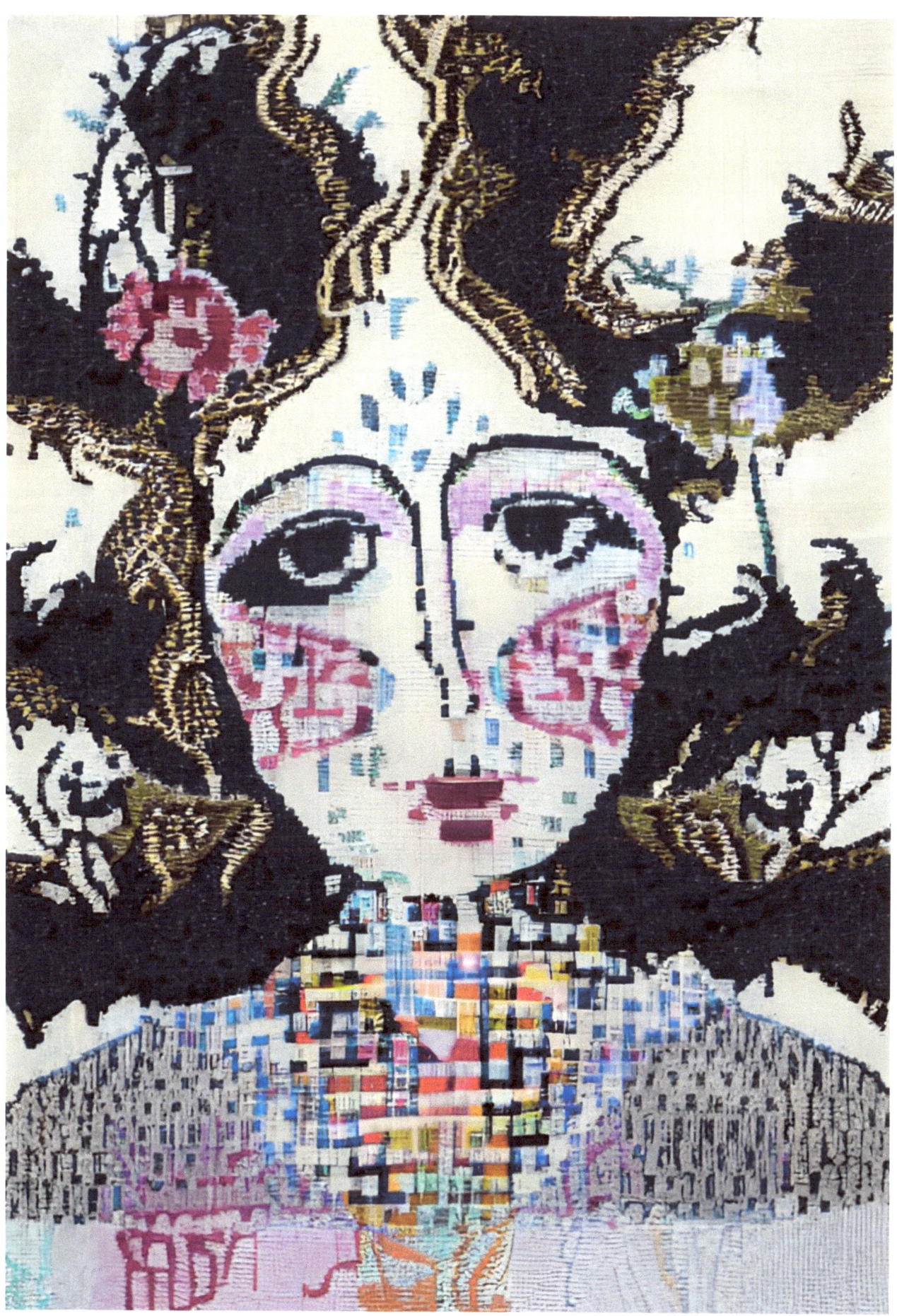

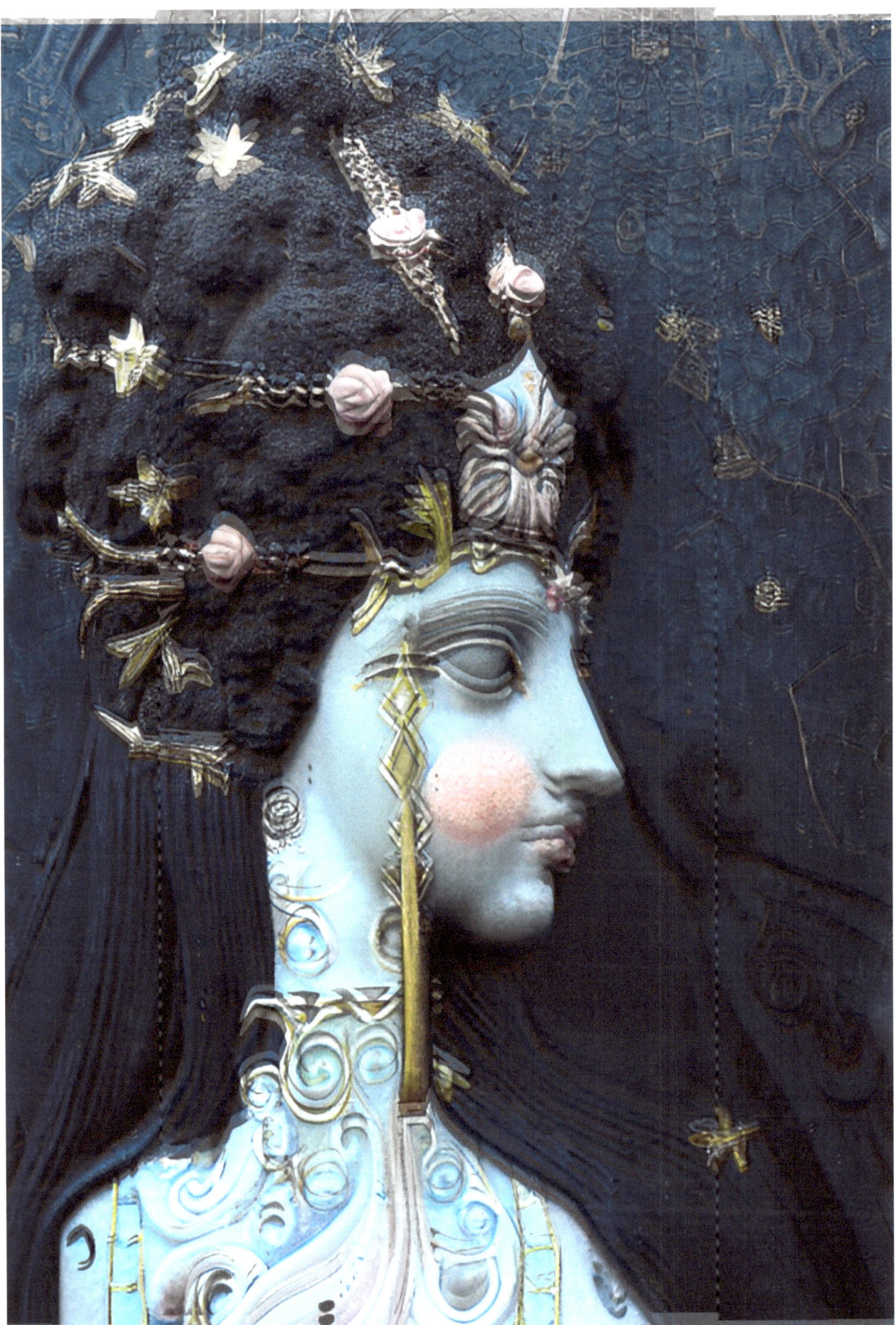

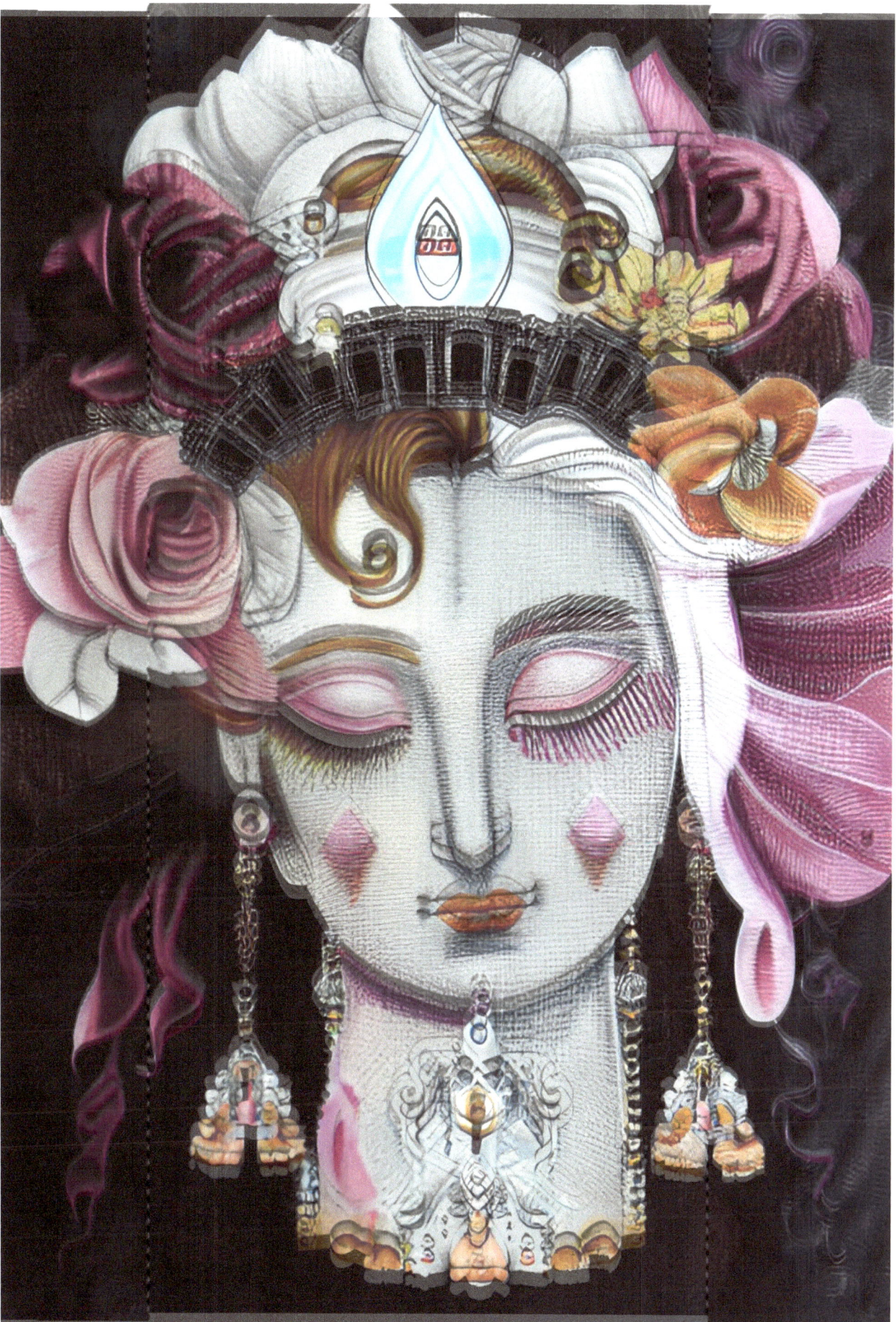

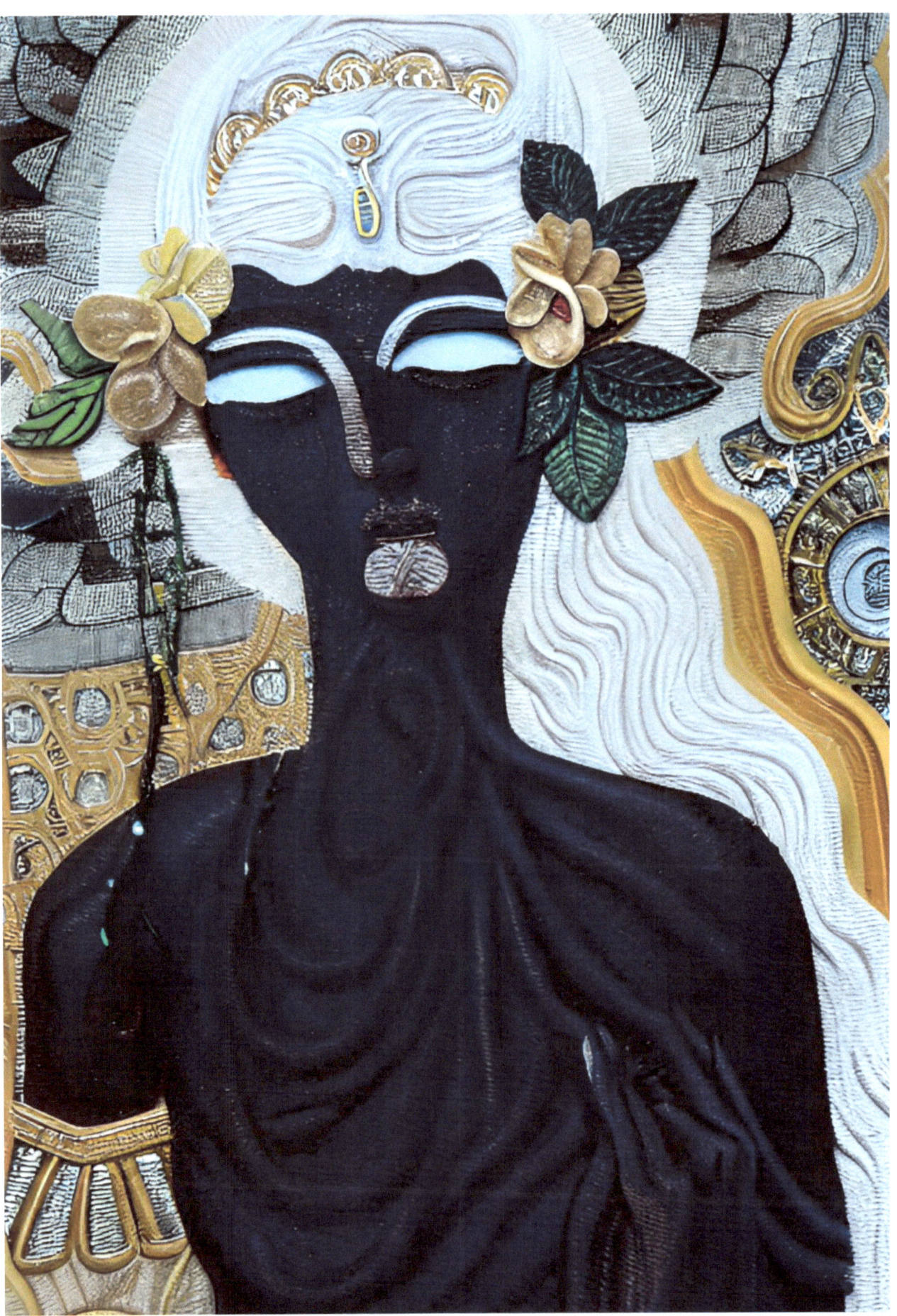

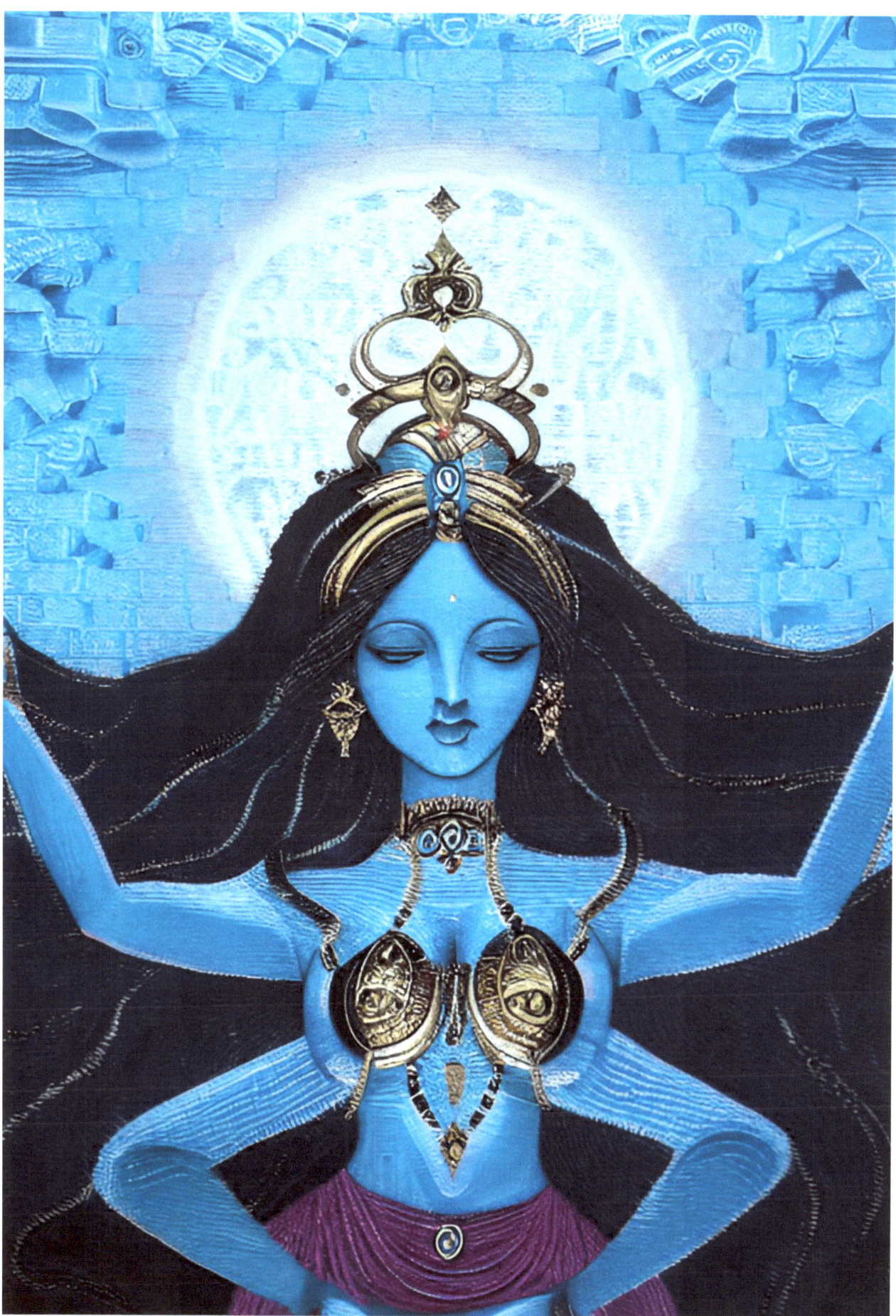

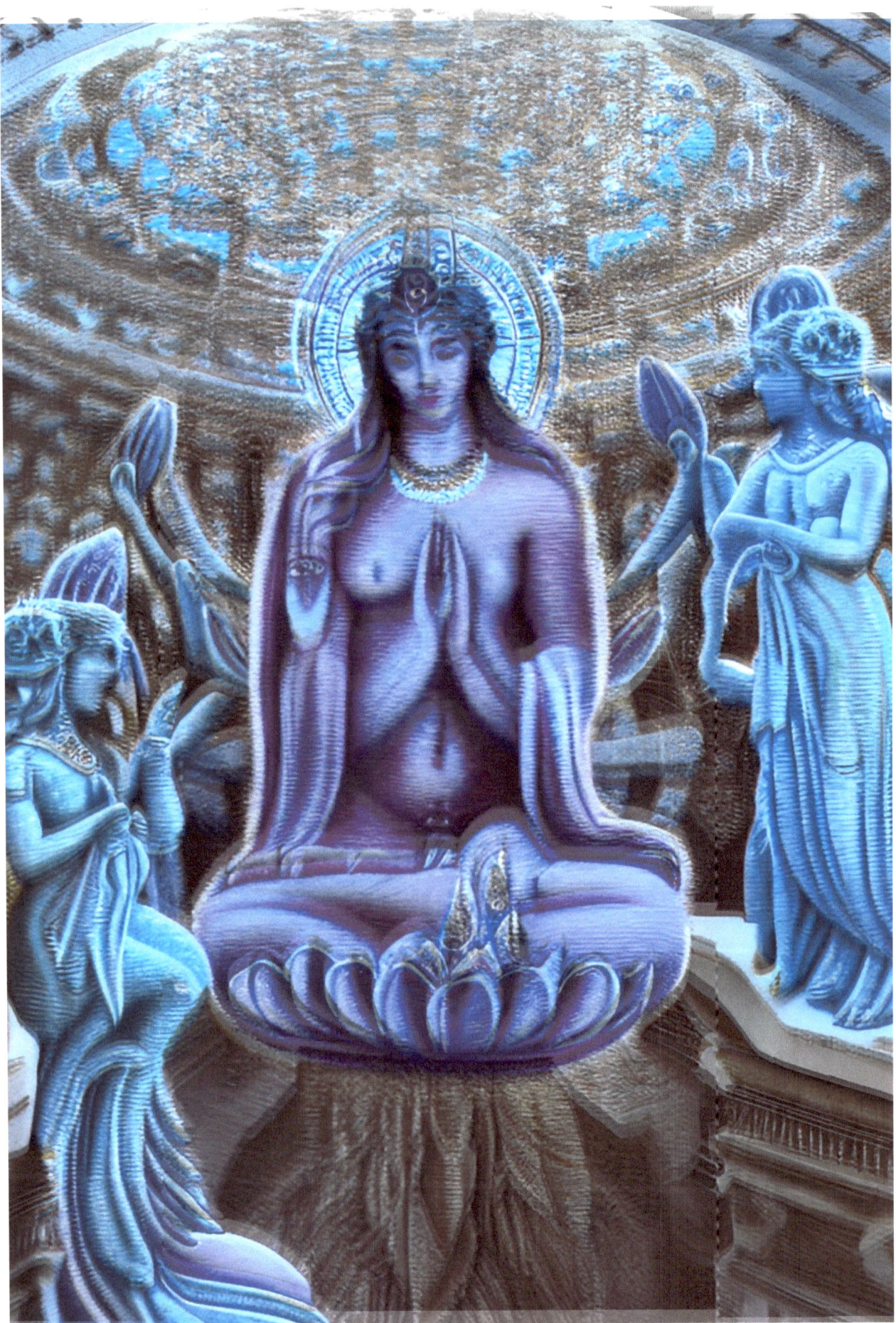

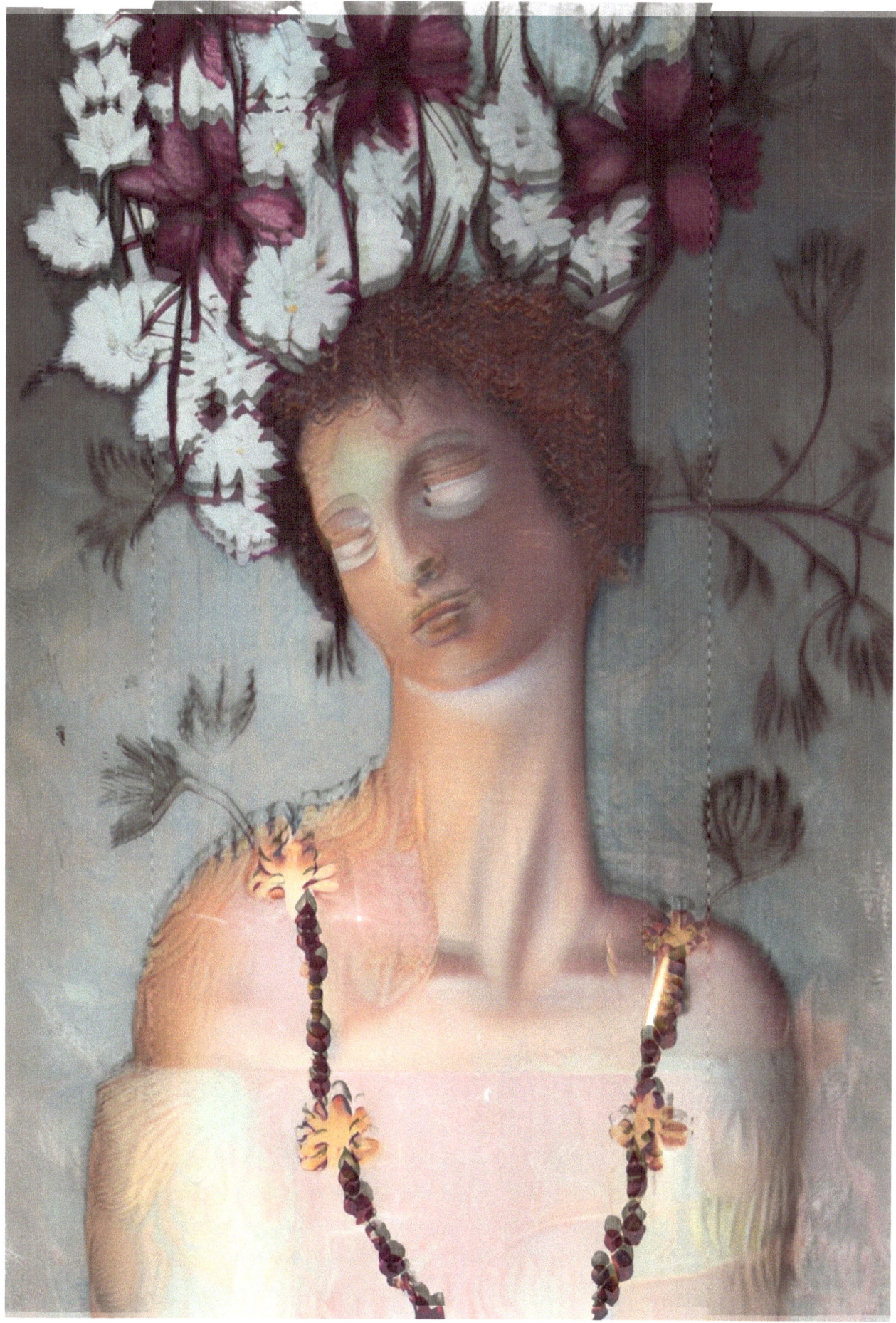

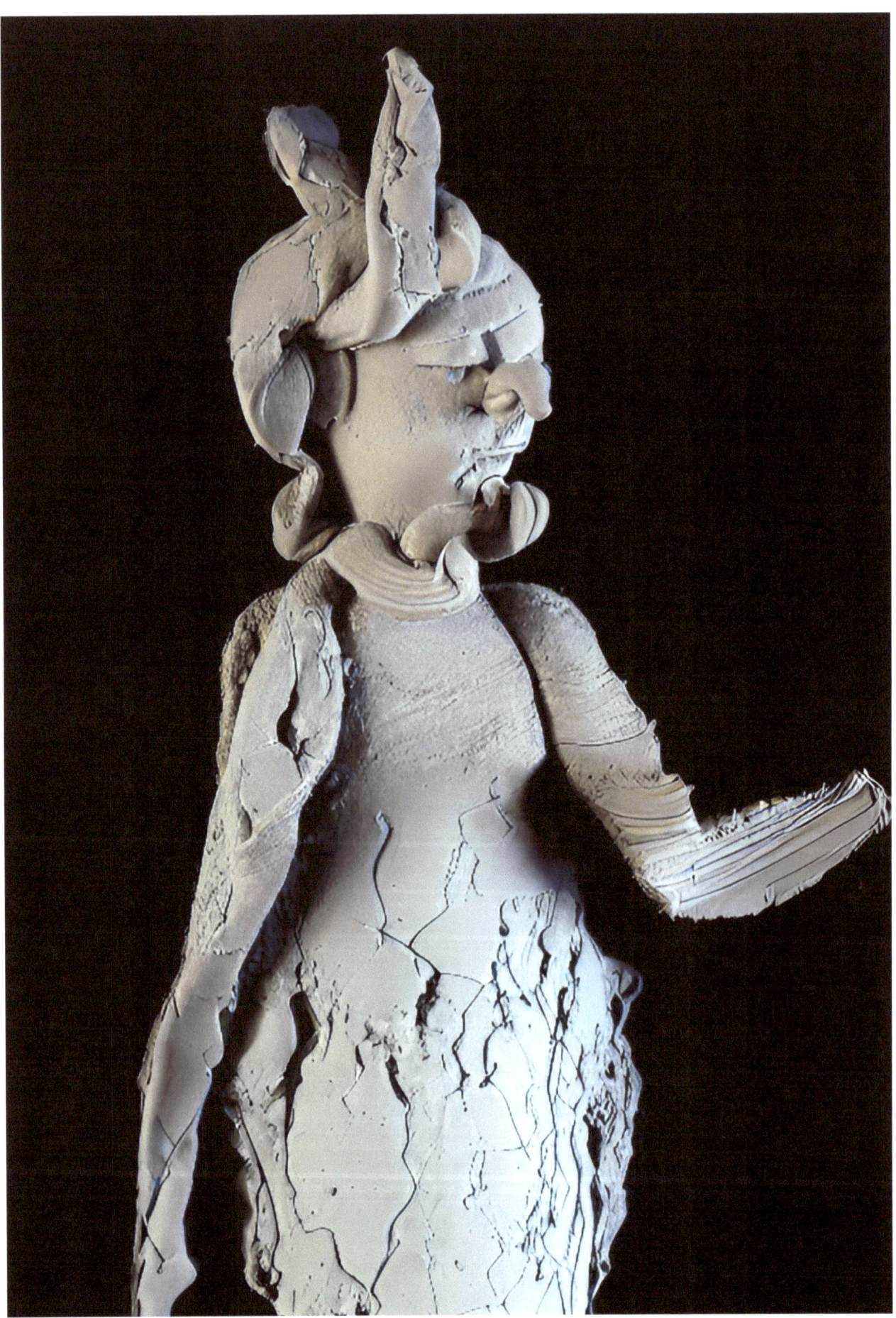

www.ingramcontent.com/pod-product-compliance
Lightning Source LLC
Chambersburg PA
CBHW051953210526
45473CB00024B/2038